Miraculous Prayers
How To Get your Miracle From God
Volume 2

Michael Blacker

www.TrueVinePublishing.org

Miraculous Prayers: Vol. 2
Michael Blacker

Published by
True Vine Publishing Co.
810 Dominican Dr.
Nashville, TN 37228

ISBN: 978-1-962783-52-1 Paperback
ISBN: 978-1-962783-58-3 eBook

Dedication

I am grateful to my parents for their lasting influence on my life.

To Dad, who is no longer with us, for teaching me the value of honesty, his hard work, focus and determination that have brought me thus far.

To Mom, whose constant love never changes despite my many imperfections.

Acknowledgments

To those who have given friendship, prayers, encouragement, various helps and finances–too many to name–I command a mighty blessing upon you which cannot be reversed in Jesus' name.

I especially want to thank my adopted family in Puerto Rico. Filiberto Cartagena Colón and Nydia León Ocasio. Pastor Martin Torres, Pastors Frankie Torres Fred and Karol S. Colón Ortiz, Pastors Jorge Cruz and Damaris Torres, Pastors Edgar Gonzalez Collazo and Elizabeth Ramírez Vega, Aida L. Vega and Cristino Del Valle. Thank you all for the special part that each one of you play in making this place my home, and helping this great Vision become a reality.

Table of Contents

Foreword

But ye shall serve the LORD your God, and he shall bless thy food and thy water; and I will take away all sickness from the midst of thee. (Exodus 23:25)

Throughout his book, Miraculous Prayers, Pastor Michael Blacker takes us on a journey of his vast experiences and how he has seen God work miracles in the lives of so many. As you read through the book, you will experience the manifest power of the Holy Spirit and the word of God working together to miraculously heal and deliver lives.

Pastor Michael is a man of God, whom the Lord has allowed us to know and love in the Love of Christ. We attest of his devotion to the Lord and love for souls. He is a servant in whom the Holy Spirit has deposited a special gift of healing. We know him certainly to be a man of prayer and unwavering faith.

Pastor Michael is a uniquely faithful witness to the Lord and has made his own the word:

It is fitting for me to declare the signs and wonders that the Most High God has done with me. (Daniel 4:2)

We highly recommend this book and know that through your reading the Holy Spirit will minister powerfully to your life and each of the testimonies shared in its pages will strengthen your faith greatly.

Blessings,

Pastor Frankie G. Fred Torres
Charismatic Christian Church
of Jesus Christ the Savior,
Villalba, Puerto Rico

Introduction

Peter therefore was kept in prison: but prayer was made without ceasing of the church unto God for him. (Acts 12:5)

How do we get miracles from God? By our prayers! Peter needed to get out of prison. King Herod had killed others, and Peter was next. The Church prayed without ceasing, and God sent an angel to bring him out of prison and save his life. Peter's miracle began with prayer.

Miracles defy natural law. When we are in an impossible situation – something that cannot be done in the natural– we need a miracle. Peter's impossibility was prison, and the hostile king determined to kill him. Life is full of impossibilities. God is a god of possibilities.

If thou canst believe, all things are possible to him that believeth (Mark 9:23).

We need to learn how to pray faith–filled prayers that overcome our impossibilities, and cause God to deliver miracles to us.

HOW DID I DISCOVER THE POTENTIAL OF PRAYER?

You are going to die – you better do something about it!

For ten years of my life, I smoked marijuana con-

11

stantly. The moment I woke up, throughout the day, and before I slept – I smoked! The final month of my ten-year addiction was a scary time for me. Like Peter in prison, death was drawing near. I was stuck in something that I had no strength to escape. For one month, every night as I lay down to sleep, I would hear a voice, which terrified me –

You are going to die – you better do something about it!

You are going to die – you better do something about it!

Thank God, my grandmother and her Church were praying for me. As a result, I found myself in Church one cold November night.

In one night, God

· Set me free of a ten – year addiction

· Healed me of all negative effects of the drug abuse

· Gave me a special gift of healing – an ability to pray for people and see Him heal them

So, I have discovered the potential of prayer. Our prayers cause God to deliver the miracles that we need in our lives. My grandmother's prayers were the first of many in my life. That memorable night in Church began a journey of more than 20 years, filled with many miracles from God. Following are some of the most memorable ones He has done.

May your faith begin to rise up as you read and learn to pray and receive miracles from God. In Jesus' name.

How to get the most from this book

Dear Reader!

How do we pray to get the miracles that we need? Very simply, there are three steps necessary to receive your miracle from God:

1. A high level of Faith
2. Biblical verses to support your petitions
3. Powerful prayers that will destroy opposition and invoke God to release a miracle.

Let's look at these three steps briefly.

A HIGH LEVEL OF FAITH

And they overcame him by . . . the word of their testimony. (Revelation 12:11)

This verse describes how the devil was overcome – *by the word of their testimony.*

God always wants to release miracles into our lives. It is the devil who doesn't want us to have them. So, according to this, one way to get them is by our testimonies. The testimonies described in this book are written with the goal of raising your faith to the high level it needs to be to receive your miracle from God.

You see, Jesus said *"All things are possible to him who believes"* (Mark 9:23)"

So, be encouraged to believe God will do the same for you. That is the first step!

BIBLICAL VERSES TO SUPPORT YOUR PETITIONS

The Bible states, *"God is not a man, that He should lie; neither the son of man, that He should repent: hath He said, and shall He not do it? or hath He spoken, and shall He not make it good?"* (Numbers 23:19).

Wow! You see, God is obligated to stand by and perform His Word. So when we find a verse to stand on, and faithfully keep it in our hearts, we have something which requires Him to deliver.

At the end of each chapter is a section entitled: **Miraculous Prayers . . .** *IN ACTION!!*

In both the testimonies, and here you will find verses to stand on for your miracle. These verses are dependable and will unfailingly work for you. Use them or find others more suitable for your own situation.

The final step to receive our miracle from God is as follows:

POWERFUL PRAYERS THAT INVOKE GOD TO RELEASE A MIRACLE

During the days of Jesus' life on earth, he offered up prayers and petitions with fervent cries and tears to the one who could save him from death, and he was heard. Hebrews 5:7 NIV

From the days of John the Baptist until now the kingdom of Heaven suffereth violence, and the violent take it by force. (Matthew 11:12)

Jesus' prayers were not quiet, and they were heard by God! Prayers that are heard by God are passionate, and often loud. Another unique quality about Jesus' ministry is His authority over the devil. Jesus fasted forty days to overcome the devil, and when He was done, He regularly casted demons out of many to perform miracles.

We need to realize we have an enemy - the devil. Regular warfare is an essential part of our passionate prayers to God. These are called *violent prayers!*

At the end of each section of **Miraculous Prayers . .** *IN ACTION* are examples of prayers you can use or model your own from these patterns.

To review, as you work towards your miracle, ask yourself the following three questions:

1. Today, as I pray, how can I increase my faith to its highest level ever?

2. Today, what Bible verse am I going to magnify in my life?

3. Today, what prayers can I make that will overcome the opposition and bring immediate victory?

This Beginning of Miracles

This beginning of miracles did Jesus in Cana of Galilee, and manifested forth His Glory; and His disciples believed on Him" (John 2:11).

I grew up in New York. My father provided very well for us. Mom stayed at home to take care of my two sisters and I. We went to a Church which my parents loved and were faithful members of for many years. Unfortunately, to us kids, it was terribly boring. It has greatly improved since then, but to us it was awful.

The rule was to continue going to Church until we were 16. As soon as my oldest sister turned 16, she stopped going. Both my younger sister and I followed her example, and also stopped going when we reached that age. Like many of my friends, I started drinking alcohol. It easily took the place in my life that was designed for the Love of God.

Unfortunately, the alcohol problem was soon taken over by drugs – marijuana. For ten years, I was addicted. Day and Night I would smoke – almost every day as long as I was able to afford it. The addiction caused me to end my education. It was taking a toll on my body – any time

I stopped, there were terrible headaches, as well as coughing up the remains that were in my chest and stomach. The only solution was to continue, in order to escape the terrible withdrawals whenever I stopped.

The drug nearly destroyed relationships with all my dear family. I lived an isolated life – my two sisters were far from me; my father was terribly angry that I had wasted the education and good life he worked so hard to provide. Mom was sad and had a hard time seeing me in this condition. My grandmother was a Christian. Although I knew little about her faith, I did know she believed in the power of prayer, and God's ability to heal. Why she was always healthy, and never needed a doctor, was a mystery to us, and something my parents never seemed to be able to explain.

At this point, she was a widow living in Florida. I saw her when she came to visit, or occasionally, I would fly to Florida. Certainly, Dad told her of my problems. Despite this, she never discussed them with me. I remember once receiving an article from her about Michael the Angel –

"There was war in Heaven: Michael and his angels fought against the dragon; and the dragon fought and his angels, and prevailed not" (Revelation 12:7, 8).

God forgive me, but I can remember my comment when I read this –

"Michael and his angels? What is this? She seems to be more stoned than I am!"

What she told me was - *God is Love*! I am praying for you. She was a perfect example of God's love whenever I visited her. She bought clothes, and gave me money, which I would use to buy drugs as soon as I reached home. Every night, I noticed the light was on in her room. When I peeped through the door– she was always studying her Bible, praying, or sitting on the bed, asleep, with her Bible in her lap.

Although it seemed very strange, a very very very tiny seed of faith was being planted in my life. I was seeing the answer that my buried heart was looking for. Little did I know that grandmother was saying the first of many miraculous prayers in my life. I was on the outside looking in – but very soon – I would be the one on the inside of this strange ritual.

Through her prayers, God was beginning His intervention in my life. While all this was happening, I heard that alarming voice every time I laid down to sleep.

"YOU ARE GOING TO DIE! YOU BETTER DO SOMETHING ABOUT IT! YOU ARE GOING TO DIE! YOU BETTER! DO SOMETHING ABOUT IT!"

How God intervened was through a friend. He was successful in business and married to a beautiful wife. Because he had both of these, when he invited me to a Bible study, I decided to go. I would like to say I went because I wanted to know more about the Bible, but that was not the reason! I thought maybe I would learn how to get a beautiful wife like him, and a successful business!

I continued in the Bible study, secretly continuing my drug habit. Eventually, the Bible Study emphasized the importance of going to Church. My friend helped me find a Church nearby, and I went to see if I liked it. On the morning before the service, I climbed the hill behind my house and got stoned. Then I went home, brushed my teeth, gargled with mouthwash, took a shower, got dressed, and went to Church!

When I arrived, they were singing beautiful songs, and praising God. Immediately, it began to touch me, and I began to cry in the presence of God. I began to visit services twice a week. Although God was doing something in my heart, I still wasn't free of the drugs. I cut down quite a bit, but because of the withdrawals, I wasn't able to get completely free. Little did I know about the beginning of miracles that were coming my way.

"This beginning of miracles did Jesus in Cana of Galilee, and manifested forth His Glory; and His disciples believed on Him" (John 2:11).

After three weeks, Jesus began His miracles in my life! He manifested His Glory, and He was about to do something that would cause me to believe on Him for the rest of my life. One cold Wednesday night in November, I attended a service. When the worship began, all of a sudden, my two hands became incredibly hot! I didn't tell anyone, but I sure didn't know what was going on! I shook them up and down to try and cool them off, but they remained so hot that they started to turn red!

As the music ended, the Pastor came to the front, and asked a very unusual question:

"Is there anyone here whose hands are hot?"

I thought to myself, what is going on here?! I raised my hand, and he called me to the front. Suddenly, I was standing beside him, with about 150 people looking at us! It was no longer just my hands – my whole body turned red from embarrassment!

I was very shy, and all the attention focused on me was too much! In the split second before the pastor spoke, I remember looking at the fire exit which was at the side of the altar. I thought to myself that I should run out and leave – that's how embarrassed I was! Then I thought again - if I ran out, I would set off the fire alarm and could never come back! I weighed the options in my mind. Although I had no idea what was about to happen, I knew I wanted to keep going to this Church, so I would have to stay put.

The pastor then explained that during the worship, **the Lord had told him** there was someone in the congregation with hot hands, and that there were also people who were sick. The Lord said the person with the hot hands (who was me) should pray for them and He would heal them! He asked if anyone was sick. Ten people raised their hands. He called them forward, and they lined up in front of us.

He then said, *"Michael, can you pray for them?"*

and held the microphone in front of my face. I covered the microphone with my hand, and whispered in his ear, *you want me to pray for them?* He nodded his head yes, and didn't say anything. I looked at the fire exit again and remembered my decision. You see, the first person in front of me was the assistant pastor - a woman. I thought to myself, *a woman? assistant pastor? I don't know how to pray! I can't pray for the pastor – I thought she was supposed to pray for me!*

It is a good thing he just shook his head, and didn't say anything, because there was no way out! I knew nothing about prayer, or the scripture,

"You shall lay hands on the sick, and they shall recover" (Mark 16:18).

I had seen the prayers at the end of each service, and the pastors and ministers put their hands on the other person, so I did the same. I placed my hand on her shoulder and simply said, *"God, can you please heal her?"*

I continued along the line, repeating the same words and putting my hand on each shoulder. When I got to the fourth person, something indescribable happened. A tremendous heat came over my whole body, and suddenly, a torrent of words came out as I prayed. As I got to the end, I touched a woman's shoulder, and before I said anything, she fell to the ground! It was a good thing that I had seen this before, because otherwise, I would have run out the fire exit for fear that I had killed someone! Amazed, I watched as the ushers laid her on the ground and covered her with a sheet! What was I doing?

I returned to my seat, feeling intoxicated. I closed my eyes, folded my hands in front of me and bowed my head. The assistant pastor came to the front of the Church and preached. I didn't hear a word of the message because I seemed to be in a state of drunkenness! Afterwards, she came up to me and thanked me for praying for her. She told me that before the prayer, she was feeling sick and was going to ask the pastor to preach instead. However, after the prayer, she got healed and preached!

I went home amazed by what had happened. God had healed her – by my prayer! Me - a struggling drug addict said six simple words - *God, can you please heal her,* and He did! It made no sense! Still feeling intoxicated, I went to sleep. The next morning, I woke up feeling the best I had ever felt in ten years! I had been set free and healed! All the headaches were gone, and the congestion had disappeared!

God had really visited me, and now I realize He changed my life in that one night. From that day, *I have never considered returning to the drugs and* have been exceptionally healthy ever since! Jesus had come into my life! After the beginning of miracles He did that night, His Glory truly manifested, and I will always believe in Him because He saved me from the death that I was certainly headed for.

ISN'T THAT WORTH SHOUTING HALLELUJAH?

We need to understand that Jesus offers both *the cure and solution* for all problems of addictions. In a world full of programs, medications, doctors, psychiatrists and therapists offering cures for addictions – may I present the only one that never fails – Jesus Christ of Nazareth!

Dear reader, if you know someone suffering with any of these problems, PLEASE! Find a Church and congregation that believes in the presence of the Holy Spirit and practices the ministry of deliverance that Jesus has entrusted to His Church even today.

MIRACULOUS PRAYERS . . . IN ACTION!

This beginning of miracles did Jesus in Cana of Galilee, and manifested forth His Glory; and His disciples believed on Him (John 2:11)

In this scripture, the ruler of the feast comments that the best wine has been brought out at the end of the feast, which was contrary to the custom of bringing it out in the beginning. I don't know where your life is, but what this means is, starting now, the remainder of it will be more exciting and intoxicating than ever before!

It is only the Power of the Holy Spirit that brings true and lasting excitement. In Acts 2, after the Holy Spirit came upon the disciples, those who stood by thought they had been drinking wine.

PRAY THIS MIRACULOUS PRAYER:

Lord Jesus:

I renounce everything called addiction. The place in my soul which was designed for the Love of God – may the Holy Spirit show up now and fill it to overflow. May a miraculous visit from the Holy Spirit change my life forever. I declare – all powers of darkness are broken. I am free. I am healed. I believe in you, and I am excited because your Glory has come and changed my life.

In Jesus' Name I pray.

A Name Above Every Name. .
The Name of Jesus

Shortly after that amazing night, I began to understand what God had done. He gives certain people gifts of healing – the ability to pray for the sick in faith, and He heals them. Very quickly, I started praying for the sick, and one of the elders of the Church began sending me to visit members in the hospital.

There was a man named Fred with Stage 4 Non-Hodgkins Lymphoma. I later discovered this is the most serious stage of the cancer, which was located in his lower back. Maybe it was better I didn't know. I just entered with the same faith I had after He had done such a wonderful miracle for me. I never considered the seriousness of the illness.

Before visiting Fred, I didn't know him very well. I discovered that he loves to talk! He can talk to anyone. There is no such thing as a short conversation with him. When I went to visit him in the hospital things were VERY DIFFERENT with both him and his wife.

As I entered the room, I knew that things were not

right. His wife, Virginia, looked VERY CONCERNED! I had never seen her looking so serious. Her usual smile and cheerful attitude were completely gone. She looked scared, and though I couldn't mention it, I imagined she was afraid she might lose her husband.

He was lying flat on the bed. She told him I had come, but he was barely awake. The chemo treatments were finished; however he was extremely dehydrated and fatigued. His normally tan Italian Complexion was completely gone, and he looked very pale. He tried to get up but couldn't. With an apology, he told me he had no strength. He showed me a full bottle of water. The doctors needed him to drink a lot of water to recover. Unfortunately, he was unable to swallow and could hardly drink at all. He faded back to sleep, and I talked to his wife briefly, but was very uncomfortable with the feelings.

Before I started to pray, I closed the door for privacy. Standing up, and closing my eyes, the same Power of God that I was beginning to know so well came over me. I raised my voice in a prayer that was full of authority. Before I knew what I was saying, something came from deep inside,

"You spirit of fear, leave now, in the name of Jesus! You spirit of death, I command you to go from this man, in the Name of Jesus! "

I ended, quite certain God was present because of what I was feeling. After opening my eyes, I saw that He had also visited both Fred and Virginia. Her eyes were full of tears. A huge smile returned to her face, she stood up and gave me a big hug!

To my amazement, he was completely awake. He fumbled to get the control and raise the back of the bed upright. After straightening up, he grabbed the full bottle of water and drank it all in one long gulp. This was amazing, but even more so was that the color of his face had come back completely.

Three days later, I received a phone call I will forever remember. It was Fred, and he was overjoyed to tell me – the doctors had released him from the hospital – Praise God! He had recovered completely, and the next CAT Scan exam confirmed what we already knew – he was completely cancer – free!

This was completely new to me. I didn't know what I was doing, but God did, and as He released the words from within, I learned how He works. I learned about the name of Jesus. In Church, they taught me – end your prayers in the name of Jesus. But in the battle, I learned WHAT HAPPENS when we end our prayers in the name of Jesus.

Wherefore God also has highly exalted Him, and given Him a name which is above every name: that at the name of Jesus every knee should bow, of things in heaven, and things in earth, and things under the earth; and that every tongue should confess that Jesus Christ is Lord, to the glory of God the Father (Philippians 3:9-11).

What happened in that room?

1. The three of us joined in faith to believe that God could heal Fred of cancer.

2. The name of Jesus was used in authority. The fear and death that were taking over their lives had to submit to the superior force represented by the name of Jesus and leave immediately.

Every time I drive by this hospital, I thank God for what He has done. I am so happy for what He has done in my life and the lives of Fred and Virginia! I smile when I remember how the devil was defeated in that place!

MIRACULOUS PRAYERS . . . *IN ACTION!*

God also has highly exalted Him, and given Him a name which is above every name: that at the name of Jesus every knee should bow, of things in heaven, and things in earth, and things under the earth. (Philippians 3:9–11).

The story of David and Goliath is well known. When the giant confronted David, he responded, *"Thou comest to me with a sword, and with a spear, and with a shield: but I come to thee in the name of the* LORD *of hosts, the God of the armies of Israel, whom thou hast defied"* (1 Samuel 17:45).

David knew the value of the name of the Lord; however you and I have that name in its perfection – the name of Jesus. I don't know what giants are in

29

your life, but what I do know is that in the Name of Jesus, they must fall.

PRAY THIS MIRACULOUS PRAYER:

Lord Jesus, have mercy on me, I pray. I command every giant which is threatening my life to fall. I speak the name above all names concerning my situation – it must submit. Giant, (name the challenge) leave my life, and die.

In the Name of Jesus.

I Shall Not Die, But Live and Declare the Works of the Lord

As I write this, I thank God for where He has brought me. For more than 10 years, I have worked full time for the Lord, and have left the various secular jobs that I worked in. It is truly exciting! However, it wasn't always that way!

Shortly after starting my Christian life, I passed through hardships I could never imagine. I reached the bottom. I felt like a prisoner in every area of my life – with no escape. There were even times I thought of ending it all – even though I had been a Christian for several years.

Living in the country with no public transportation, a car is essential. The old car I had for several years broke down almost every month, draining my finances. Eventually the motor blew up, leaving me completely stranded. At the same time, all work seemed to stop, and I had no way to even look for

31

work. Bills went unpaid for months, and it was a challenge to keep the phone from being cut off. I was at an all-time low – struggling to keep enough food in the house.

In addition, sickness began to attack me. After receiving the gift of healing, one of the benefits seemed to be excellent health. The scripture says,

Pray for others that you may be healed. (James 5:16)

Apparently one of the special benefits of working in a healing ministry is that God keeps me healthy. Although there have been occasional challenges along the way, I have come to know and trust that the Lord is always faithful to completely heal me.

Yet, all of a sudden, this divine health came under attack. I developed a painful case of hemorrhoids which would not go away.

The Lord will smite thee with emerods (hemorrhoids) (Deuteronomy 28:27)

In the Bible, hemorrhoids are described as one of the curses of the law. I asked myself – *why has this curse come upon me?* The medication, which didn't seem to work, had a terrible smell which was like a black cloud following me all day long. Besides this, the nerves in my right foot became numb. I walked with a limp - the foot wouldn't lift, and I had to drag it along with every step. This further added to my depression because all my life I have loved exercise – running, or walking is almost as essential to me as breathing. I began to feel like a crippled old man shuffling along.

Finally, I was a frustrated Christian.

*Faith, if it has not works, is dead. (*James 2:17)

I had spent almost ten years sitting in Church hearing the Word of God, experiencing the move of the Holy Spirit, but I HAD NO MINISTRY! Occasionally I prayed for the sick, and saw God heal them, but not on a regular basis. The gift I had was stagnant. Proverbs 13:12 says,

Hope deferred eventually makes the heart sick.

That was me–tired of just sitting in Church and becoming more hopeless every day. Everything changed when I discovered one line of scripture:

*I shall not die, but live and declare the works of the Lord (*Psalm 118:17).

Something within me began to fight again when I discovered this verse. I decided I was going to resist these feelings of darkness. I began to confess it day and night. I began to repeat continually . . .

"I *shall not die, but live and declare the works of the Lord . . . .*

I shall not die, but live and declare the works of the Lord . . . .

I shall not die, but live and declare the works of the Lord. "

I even made a song out of it. Nothing happened immediately on the outside, but SOMETHING was going on within me. I felt lifted up. I knew that I would live.

THE WALLS OF THE PRISON I WAS IN CAME CRASHING DOWN AT THIS MOMENT.

I knew in The Spirit that I would be alright. Death was behind me. After a while, things began happening - amazingly, a good friend gave me a beautiful car - with four-wheel drive! He took it to the mechanic for a tune up, paid for two months of insurance, and gave me the keys! Gradually I began to get work and income to meet my needs. My health improved, and I received complete healing in my body.

Finally, I was accepted into a Chaplaincy program at a local hospital where I could visit the sick on a regular basis. I now had a ministry. Even now it is difficult to describe the great satisfaction that comes from praying for the sick and seeing the touch of God upon their lives. I knew that I would not die. I knew that I would live and declare the works of the Lord.

PART 2

Several months after starting the program, someone referred me to a man in the Intensive Care Unit. (ICU) This was only my second visit to the ICU. I knew it was a serious place and felt a bit nervous going in because of how critical some of the patients were. Let me explain:

A patient I knew from the rehabilitation unit got

worse and was transferred to the ICU. So, I visited him there. I found the ICU, and discovered the two security doors were locked. Unlike other units, this required permission to enter. I was even more surprised when I swiped my badge in front of the sensor, and the doors automatically opened!

I headed to the nurse's station to ask permission to visit the patient in Room 906. As I approached, the nurse was on the phone. I got close to her, and what I overheard almost sent me running right out the two doors again. I heard her saying, *can you send someone up to take a body to the morgue? We have a patient who has expired in Room 90 . . .*

The split second before I heard the final number seemed like the longest moment in my life. She said, *can you send someone up to take a body to the morgue? We have a patient who has expired in Room 907.* I finally breathed again when I realized the dead patient was in the room next to the one I was going to visit. I visited the patient in 906, and it went well.

However, what I learned was very real, and way too close. The ICU is a place of life and death. Shortly after this, I returned to the ICU. Can you imagine how I felt visiting again? On this Wednesday night, I entered the patient's room and saw him lying on the bed UNRESPONSIVE, with his head on the pillow, and eyes closed – in a coma.

Life support was attached – a respirator, a tube in

his throat, and dialysis machine were keeping him alive. I didn't know why he was there. I spoke for a few minutes, assuming he heard me - although he did not respond. Finally, I said, *Brother if you can hear me move your hand!* To my surprise, I saw his hand move slightly underneath the sheet! I said to God,

OK this is enough to work with!

Immediately The Spirit of the Lord told me what to tell him. Can you guess? I put my face next to his ear, and yelled into his ear,

Brother, you shall not die, you shall live and declare the works of the Lord!

I shouted again, *Brother, you shall not die, you shall live and declare the works of the Lord!* After several minutes, I ended my prayer and left. Nothing visible had happened, and he remained unresponsive. Four days later, on a Sunday Afternoon, I returned. As I entered, and looked into the room, I froze. I could not move. What I saw caused me to stop. In the middle of the hallway, God caused me to freeze. John wrote in Revelation 1:10 –

I was in The Spirit on the Lord's day . .

This is exactly what happened to me. Instantly, I was in ANOTHER DIMENSION. That is why I froze. When I looked into the room, and saw God's answer to my prayer, I entered into The Spirit. It became a different place. For several minutes I was in the middle of a busy hallway in the ICU, having an intimate moment with God, yet not a single person appeared, or disturbed me. God stepped in and visited me.

I closed my eyes and began to cry uncontrollably for several minutes! When I finally opened them again, I beheld the same man. He was sitting up in the bed! All life support was off his face, and his eyes were open. He was eating dinner and watching TV! He looked at me uncertainly, not knowing who I was. I began to say, *Hallelujah, Hallelujah, Hallelujah! Thank You, Jesus!* As I said this, I heard him answering me. The tubes had damaged his vocal cords, but I heard him in a gravelly kind of voice answering me, *Thank You, Jesus! Praise the Lord!*

After we praised The Lord together for a minute or two, I entered the room and introduced myself. For several weeks, I visited regularly. He was 53 and had spent most of his life drinking alcohol. Before our meeting, he had suffered massive kidney failures. In one and a half weeks, on five different occasions, his kidneys had completely shut down! It was a miracle that he was not brain dead from this.

I saw great improvements every time I came back. He began to talk better, his mind was absolutely clear, and he walked better every week. Toward the end of his stay, when I came to his room, quite often he wasn't there. He would return shortly, always excited to see me. He had been visiting other patients and telling them what the Lord had done for him!

Several weeks after his discharge, we went to Church together. He was very proud to tell me how much his life had improved, and that he was completely free of alcohol! As we both shared testimony in the Church, all realized that the faithful promise of God had come to pass in his life.

I shall not die, but live and declare the works of the Lord.

PART 3

After a while in the hospital, The Lord directed me to start working at a Christian Drug and Alcohol Rehabilitation Center for a few hours a week. After counseling one of the residents for several months, the director invited me to come to their Friday Chapel Service and Preach. Before this Friday, I spent most of the previous week fasting and praying. I felt very close to the Spirit of God when I shared the message.

I recorded the message and noticed something very interesting when I listened to it later. At one point, I stopped and announced to the audience - I have a word from God for someone, *"you have been wondering if you are going to make it through this – if you can ever put your life back together - you have even thought of ending it. I declare the Word of God to you today - you shall not die, you shall live and declare the works of the Lord."*

Several months went by. I produced this CD, and

even shared it with some of my friends. I often wondered about the person who was supposed to hear this word from the Lord. One day, I went to visit again. After seeing some of the staff, I went downstairs to visit a few residents who were working out in the basement. After a while, I said goodbye and started to leave. As I climbed the stairs, I heard a soft voice – so soft, I thought I was imagining it – but it made me stand still -

I shall not die, but live and declare the works of The Lord!

I stopped. Seeing a man seated nearby, I asked what he had said.

I shall not die, but live and declare the works of The Lord! he replied!

I asked where he got that from, and he said – *you prayed it over me!* I was so excited to hear that! Months later he remembered the word, and it had worked in his life!

I shall not die, but live and declare the works of the Lord.

I know in Heaven; King David rejoices every time he hears his Psalm and celebrates another victory over death! It has worked in my life, and Glory to God, in the lives of many others!

MIRACULOUS PRAYERS . . . *IN ACTION!*

I shall not die, but live and declare the works of the

Lord. Psalm 118:17

In this verse, there are three progressive steps –

1.Confronting the forces of death

2.Receiving New Life from the Spirit of the Lord

3.Going to work for God

When God does a miracle for us, it is for His Glory, and He wants us to tell others.

PRAY THIS MIRACULOUS PRAYER:

Lord Jesus, I destroy every spirit of death that is troubling me. I command - leave me now forever. Holy Spirit, I ask you to come and breathe new life upon me. May the Resurrection Power of the Lord Jesus Christ fill me now. What the enemy planned for evil has now been changed for good; my life will become a testimony of the wonderful works of The Lord. I will tell others what He has done for me! I boldly declare,

I shall not die, but live and declare the works of the Lord.

In Jesus' Name

Children Playing in the Streets

After working in the hospital for a while, I met a lot of elderly patients. After several experiences with patients either before, during or after their deaths, I began to consider what happens after life on earth. This forced me to draw closer to God. What I saw convinced me that there is truly a Heaven, and a hell.

Why do I say this? One patient would be in continual torment as the end of life drew near. Another would be at perfect peace. Shortly after, they passed away. I realized it is a great privilege to see what the end of the road is like. I began to dig deep into God, and the Bible to learn about Heaven and hell.

I found two scriptures about Heaven that fascinated me:

But ye are come unto mount Zion, and unto the city of the living God, the heavenly Jerusalem, and to an innumerable company of angels (Hebrews 12:22).

Thus says the Lord: I shall return to Zion and will dwell in the midst of Jerusalem, and Jerusalem shall be called the [faithful] City of Truth, and the mountain of the Lord of hosts, the Holy Mountain. Thus says the Lord of hosts: Old men and old women shall again dwell in Jerusalem and sit out in the streets, every man with his staff in his hand for very [advanced] age. **And the streets of the city shall be full of boys and girls playing in its streets** (Zechariah 8:3 - 5).

As I studied, it fascinated me to discover something about family in the Bible – the relationship of the elderly and children. It is evident that the elderly have a very important role in the lives of the children. They are together – sitting in the streets, watching over the children as they play.

Old men and old women shall again dwell in Jerusalem and sit out in the streets, every man with his staff in his hand for very [advanced] age. **And the streets of the city shall be full of boys and girls playing in its streets.**

What I saw in the hospital was completely different than the Bible. Most of the elderly were all alone – frequently with little or no family contact. I perceived something from this – the elderly have a place of honor in the family. Especially towards the end of life it is not God's design for them to be far from each other. Thus it is written –

With long life will I satisfy him and show him my salvation. (Psalm 91:16)

The biblical image of elderly in a place of honor, caring for children playing in the streets stayed with me, and made me understand how important family is to God, and in Heaven. While with the hospital, I also worked as a taxi driver. One day I went to pick up an elderly American woman and her caregiver, who was from the Philippines.

I got to know them and took them to the doctor almost every week. The woman had Alzheimer's disease and was having a lot of trouble with her mind. The caregiver was a lovely lady and showed such tenderness that I really admired her. Although it was sad, I looked forward to seeing them both. One day, I went, and the caregiver came out alone. She was very sad and told me why.

I am worried about her - she sits all day, looking at the tree outside the window. She is very happy, but keeps saying over and over, **Oh, they're playing! The Children are playing!**

Before even thinking about it, I said something. What I said came out from a place in me that I didn't even know about, because it came out so quickly. The reply didn't come from my mind – it came from the Spirit within me. I said,

Don't worry, she is getting ready to die and go to Heaven!

The lady looked at me with a puzzled look on her face. We talked about the scripture, and immediately, a great peace came over her. Before parting, I prayed for both of them and asked God to have mercy upon

43

the woman and receive her life. A week later, I was sent, and again she came out alone. She began to cry when she saw me. Her dear employer had passed away, and this day was the funeral.

She also explained that she was returning to her home in the Philippines! She had taken care of this woman fifteen years – her one and only job in the United States. Now that she had passed, it was time to return home. It was a great honor to share this special moment in the lives of these two women.

Certainly, our meetings were ordained by God. I did not discuss any of this with the dispatcher, yet out of the usual 5 drivers available, I was the one that was always sent. We had a moving prayer at the train station, and I said goodbye to one woman as she made her way home to the Philippines. I said goodbye to the other as she made her way home to Heaven! HALLE-LUJAH!

MIRACULOUS PRAYERS . . . IN ACTION!

But ye are come unto mount Zion, and unto the city of the living God, the heavenly Jerusalem, and to an innumerable company of angels (Hebrews 12:22)

Thus says the Lord of hosts: Old men and old women shall again dwell in Jerusalem and sit out in the streets, every man with his staff in his hand for very advanced age. And the streets of the city shall be full of boys and girls playing in its streets. (Zechariah 8:3–5)

Few people nowadays have an ideal family situation, a strong support system among the two, three or even four generations of their family living together. If you are one of those, I am sure you are very grateful to God.

Whatever our family situation is, God's Grace is available from Heaven to help us.

PRAY THIS MIRACULOUS PRAYER –

Lord Jesus –

I come to Heavenly Jerusalem now, bringing my family before you. Forgive me of my sins. I now receive Your Grace to help mend and heal every broken situation in my family. I ask you for eternal life. May Heaven bless me today. I commit my life and my family to you forever.

In Jesus' Name I pray

Let Us Pass to the Other Side

When I met James in the hospital, he was very anxious and concerned about his wife. Recovering from a shoulder injury, she was alone, and their children were not helping as they should have. Doing her usual physical work of cooking, cleaning, and even bathing was not possible with the weak shoulder, and he was afraid she might hurt herself trying to do some of these things.

I asked why he was in the hospital because he was not talking about it. To my surprise, his leg had swollen to almost 1 ½ times normal, due to diabetes. There was infection in several toes, which the doctors were investigating. They had mentioned a possible surgery which would cut his leg open. With this would come a high risk of future infection, and a very slow healing process due to poor blood circulation and diabetes.

After listening carefully, and talking, we discussed a passage where Jesus calms the sea.

And the same day, when the even was come, He

*said to them, **Let us Pass Over Unto the Other Side.** And when they had sent away the multitude, they took Him even as He was in the ship. And there were also with Him other little ships. And there arose a great storm of wind, and the waves beat into the ship, so that it was now full. And He was in the hinder part of the ship, asleep on a pillow; and they awoke Him, and said to Him, Master, carest thou not that we perish? And He arose, and rebuked the wind, and said unto the sea, **Peace, be still.** And the wind ceased, and there was a great calm and He said unto them, why are you so fearful? How is it that you have no faith? And they feared exceedingly, and said one to another, what manner of man is this, that even the wind and the sea obey Him?* (Mark 4:35-41)

I started to pray and brought this into the prayer. I asked God to calm every storm, and bring James and his family to the other side of Peace and stillness. I made a bold declaration, and said,

Let us pass over to the other side ...

I asked God to heal his leg, restore it to normal, and for there to be no complications, or side effects in the doctor's treatments. We asked that his wife's mind would be set at ease, and the family would join together to help with the housework so she could recover. James thanked me, and I sensed a great calm. Two days later, when I visited him, he repeated my message –

Let us pass over to the other side!

He was completely changed – there were no signs of anxiety. I knew he had reached the other side of Peace. Happily, he showed me his leg. The morning after our prayer, he got out of bed and walked easily for the first time in several days! The swollen leg which could barely bend, was almost completely normal, and now was able to bend almost fully!

One week later, a minor procedure was done. He was happy to show me the leg, which was completely normal. The two-step procedure was as follows – by injecting fluid into his leg, they discovered two veins that were clogged behind the knee. In the second step, the blockage was removed in a way that did not require cutting his leg open.

James was very happy that no surgery was necessary and was recovering very well. He was also happy that everything was fine at home. The children were all working together and taking good care of Mom. As a team, with God, doctors, nurses, staff of the hospital, and his now united family, I was happy to see . . .

James and his family have passed over to the other side!

Thank God for bringing him to the other side of the storm. Mom is at peace now, and the family has come together to take care of her. His leg has returned to normal, with no side effects or complications.

MIRACULOUS PRAYERS . . . *IN ACTION!*

*And He arose, and rebuked the wind, and said unto the sea, **Peace, be still**. And the wind ceased, and there was a great calm and He said unto them, why are you so fearful? How is it that you have no faith?*

And they feared exceedingly, and said one to another, what manner of man is this, that even the wind and the sea obey Him? (Mark 4:35–41)

How they marveled at the authority of Jesus to order the wind and sea to obey. Joshua commanded the Sun and Moon to stand still so the army of Israel could avenge themselves of their enemies. Both Jesus and Joshua knew the authority that they had.

PRAY THIS MIRACULOUS PRAYER:

Lord Jesus:

I declare I will pass over to the other side of my destiny. Sun, moon, earth, water, sky, wind and forest you must now work in my favor. I now command every storm of my life to be silent and cease now. I will be still, and know that you are God, the Creator of the Heavens and the Earth. By your mighty Power I will reach my destiny.

In Jesus' Name

I Will Take Sickness from Your Midst

One night I visited an elderly man who was recovering from hip replacement surgery. He was in a good frame of mind and felt very well, except for severe constipation. The hip area was very tender, and he had been unable to relieve himself. He was not walking yet, and without exercise, his digestion seemed to have stopped.

He was eating well since his surgery, but was unable to relieve himself, and it was causing him a lot of pain. His belly did look rather swollen. When we discussed God, he told me how devoted he was, and I sensed that he really loved the Lord. As we prepared to pray, I remembered an experience from years before and told him . . .

Not long after becoming a Christian, I had to have my appendix removed. My whole mid-section was very painful and tender. During recovery, I had terrible gas and was unable to get relief. When I was discharged from the hospital, the stomach was very bloated, and they told me I needed to pass gas in order to get an ease. Exercise would help greatly, so I began to walk more every day as I gained strength.

I was staying with my parents for a few days, until I could take care of myself. The first night I came home we were all in the living room. They were watching TV, and I laid down on the couch to relax. While laying down, I began to pray quietly and meditate. My stomach was still bloated, and very uncomfortable.

As I prayed, I began to concentrate on the stomach muscles, and moved them, starting at the top, gradually going all the way down to the bowel area. All of a sudden, two days' build up of gas left, and there was a loud sound—'PFFFFFFFFFFFTTTT". I shouted Hallelulah!! I felt the wonderful relief immediately. We all began to laugh, and my parents began to clap enthusiastically!

Not too long after this great relief, I was reading the Bible.

You shall serve the Lord your God: He shall bless your bread and water, and I will take sickness away from the midst of thee (Exodus 23:25)

As I thought about this, I realized this is exactly what had happened to me! There is a blessing from the Lord upon whatever enters our bodies. Because of that blessing, sickness is taken away, and our digestive systems are restored to health. Even more special about this was this part.

I will take sickness away from the midst of thee

In one loud passage of gas, this promise became a revelation to me. He indeed took sickness from my mid-section that day! Amen? As I understood this more, I began to make it a regular prayer before eating,

The Lord shall bless my food and water, and He shall take sickness from the midst of me.

Now I am sure you know what we prayed that night:

You shall serve the Lord your God: He shall bless your food and water, and I will take sickness away from the midst of thee

The presence of God really came, and tears came down the man's face. By the end, we both were laughing hysterically. It seemed that God had touched us both in a special way. I said goodbye and stepped outside the room. Right outside was a friend of mine who was this patient's nurse. She was working at her computer station. I stopped and talked with her. Because the door was open, I was sure she had heard the prayer, and from her smile, I knew it had touched her too.

Within less than 1 minute, we heard a loud alarm go off within the room. She ran in, knocking her papers all over the floor. Another nurse came running down the hall to help and went in, shutting the door. I waited outside, not knowing what was going on. However, because the presence of God was so beautiful, I just began to thank Him for visiting us. I was very confident that everything was OK. I waited until they came out to discover what happened.

After a few minutes, my friend came out and told me. There was an alarm attached to the patient because he was considered *high risk.* There was a risk of injury to his hip if he were to fall out of bed, or to get out unassisted. The man was VERY SURPRISED when suddenly he had an extremely large bowel movement! In desperation, he had tried to get to the bathroom, which set off the alarm.

I was happy to know that they cleaned him up, and everything was OK. Most of all, an immediate answer had come to our prayer for relief. This convinced me that without question, The Lord is able to . .

Bless our food and water, and take sickness from the midst of us!

MIRACULOUS PRAYERS . . . IN ACTION!

You shall serve the Lord your God: He shall bless your bread and water, and I will take sickness away from the midst of thee (Exodus 23:25)

This is a simple formula: God doesn't require so much from us – just a few simple things.

When God did a miracle, and sent manna from Heaven, the Israelites complained and lusted for the foods they ate in Egypt. In Numbers 11, we see that

God destroyed them. We must learn to be thankful for what He has given us to eat. We serve the Lord by taking a few moments to thank Him and bless our food before we eat.

For many of us, our diets, and health would be much better if we practiced this custom – bless our food before eating.

PRAY THIS MIRACULOUS PRAYER:

Lord Jesus:

Thank you for this food you have given me. I examine my life, and I am thankful to you. Forgive my sins. I present my body to you as the Temple of the Holy Ghost. I will serve you. Use this food and water to drive out every sickness and restore health to my body.

In Jesus' Name

Seeing is Believing

There was a young man in the Hospital who was 22 years old. I first met him in the rehabilitation unit. Ron was in the ICU for six weeks until he finally improved enough to be moved to rehab. It was amazing to hear his story. He used alot of drugs and alcohol. Unfortunately, he had a bad car accident while drinking and hit a tree head on. Although the seat belt was on, his head hit the steering wheel, and his brain was badly injured. As a result, he was in a coma for six weeks.

Many of the doctors did not expect him to ever come out of the coma. However, thank God, he did. Shortly after this, he moved to rehab, where we met. Ron grew up in Church, and knew about the things of God, but had fallen into drugs and alcohol. So, when he came out of the coma, and realized that God had spared him, he was very grateful. He had a renewed outlook on life, and great faith in God. It was exciting to hear him talk about how God had rescued him from near death.

Due to the accident, he suffered partial brain damage. As a result, he walked unsteadily, and his eyesight was cloudy. He was able to see things close up, but the background was always cloudy. In addition to this, he had become cross eyed. When I made eye contact with him, one eye looked directly at me, but the other looked in a different direction.

Because he was in rehab for several months, we met often. He really looked forward to seeing me, and talking about God, and the Bible. Our prayers helped him get through many challenges. One night, we had an extended prayer, where the presence of God came in a beautiful way. Before the prayer, I remember thinking how hard it was to look at the two eyes going in different directions.

After the prayer, tears were running down both of our faces. As he opened his eyes, there was a puzzled look on his face. When he looked at me, I was amazed! Both eyes were looking directly at me! His erratic eye had been corrected! Ron, still kind of puzzled, said to me,

I don't believe it, but I seem to be seeing better! the cloudiness is gone! I am seeing clearly!

I told him that both of his eyes were now focused perfectly. We had witnessed a miracle! We both were amazed by what had taken place. For both of us, this was such a surprise! It was a very special, yet unusual moment. We were both a little unsure as we realized that God had come into the room with us.

Psalm 126:1 describes the feeling well –

When the Lord turned the captivity of Zion, we were like them that dreamed.

After being captive for a long time, when freedom came to Zion, it felt unreal – like a dream. That is how we felt. We laughed about his reaction; *I don't believe it!* I understood his reaction, because it had happened to me before. When the answer to our prayer arrives – we often say, *I don't believe it!* How awesome when our unbelieving selves get a miracle! I remembered what Jesus said when He appeared to Thomas and the disciples after His resurrection *Because you have seen me, you have believed; blessed are those who have not seen and yet have believed.* (John 20:29)

We were both so surprised to have his sight restored, but I know one thing for certain–we now believe!

MIRACULOUS PRAYERS. ..*IN ACTION!*

Because you have seen me, you have believed; blessed are those who have not seen and yet have believed. (John 20:29)

There is a famous Minister I know. When I listen to his story, I frequently hear him say, *from the beginning, whenever I prayed, I saw myself speaking to thousands of people!* Now he travels the world preaching the Gospel and has visited hundreds of countries working for the Kingdom. But from his humble beginning in Africa, it wasn't always so.

What is your heart's desire? What do you long to accomplish in your life? Can you see it? When you close your eyes, can you taste, feel, hear, smell and even touch what it will be like when it comes?

PRAY THIS MIRACULOUS PRAYER:

Lord Jesus, forgive me of unbelief. I command every spirit of unbelief to leave my life. I am changed. I believe You rose from the dead, and are alive forevermore. By the same power that raised you from the dead, I call to life my miracle. I see it coming to pass. I can hear it. I can smell it, I can even taste it. All things are possible to him that believes – that is me!

In Jesus' Name

He Shall Give His Angels Special Charge Over Thee

A thousand may fall at your side, and ten thousand at your right hand, but it shall not come near you . . .

*For He shall give His angels especial charge over thee . . . (*Psalm 91:7,11 Amplified)

I say a regular prayer every morning when I get into my car. There are three verses which always keep me safe and ensure my daily prosperity. They are as follows –

*The Lord shall keep thee from all evil. The Lord shall preserve thy soul. The Lord shall preserve my going out and my coming in from this time forth and even forever more. (*Psalm 121:7, 8)

The Glory of the Lord shall be my rereward. (Isaiah 58:8)

My God shall supply all your need according to His riches in Glory by Christ Jesus. (Philippians 4:19)

As I drive away, I say this prayer for the day ahead. I meditate on it as I go along, and cover whatever I have planned for the day. Occasionally, when I get in the car, I hear within myself – *read Psalm 91!* I usually hear this when I am late or leaving in a hurry. I recognize this voice now, and obey it, because it is the Lord telling me there is danger ahead, and He needs a few minutes to protect me. Also, my heart needs to be calm before I leave and face the day ahead. I obey, take out my Bible, and read Psalm 91 slowly, and with conviction.

This Psalm is a great promise of God's protection. After reading it, I am always focused and at peace. Often there is danger out on the road. However, without fail, God protects me and always brings me home safely.

A thousand may fall at your side, and ten thousand at your right hand, but it shall not come near you. Only with thine eyes shall thou behold and see the reward of the wicked. V 7,8

Having driven a taxi for several years, I have seen many car accidents, and often feel a leading to turn off and follow a different route, only to discover that there was some sort of accident in the place I avoided. At first, seeing accidents occur scared me, but when I realized the significance of the above verse, I realized how very real God's protection is in my life. Accidents suffered by others, yet escaped by me, are evidence that God is with me as I go out each day to do His will.

For He shall give His angels especial charge over

thee...

Now, when I feel a leading to go a certain way which appears longer, or more inconvenient, I stop resisting with my logical mind. I realize that God's angels are at work protecting my travels. Exodus 23:20 reinforces this:

Behold, I send an Angel before thee, to keep thee in the way, and to bring thee into the place which I have prepared.

There was a time I left the hospital where I was working. I said goodbye to all my friends, because I was planning to enroll in a program at a different hospital. As things turned out, I returned to the hospital 6 months later. However, I will always remember the first night I returned – it was a bitter cold night in January.

The night before, I drove to the parking lot which is on a hill overlooking the hospital. I spent 2 or 3 hours in my car praying regarding my future work there – that was how special this was for me – I decided to consecrate it with a long time of prayer! So, when I returned, I was very happy, and very full of the presence of God! Of course, because I had said goodbye to everyone, and did not expect to return, they were all very surprised to see me again. It was a night full of happiness, and many hugs, which I really enjoyed.

When I am at work in the hospital, I am usually

full of the Holy Spirit. I lose track of time and become full of energy. However, when it is time to stop, I *return to earth*. Often it is late, and suddenly I realize how tired I am! This first night was like that. Because of the previous night's prayer, the high level of emotions, and the joy of returning to a place I love, I went over my limit of physical endurance. When I decided to go home, all the excitement and enthusiasm caught up with me! I drove home, and though I was praying, singing and worshipping God – I was really tired!

Because of this, I was not as attentive as I should have been. As I neared my house, there was a patch of ice on the road that I did not see. Immediately, the car began to slide sideways across the other lane, heading straight into a ditch. As I noticed this, I had no time to react by moving the steering wheel, but what came out of my mouth immediately was a cry for help – JE-SUS!

As the car slid sideways on the ice toward the ditch, I immediately felt it change direction! The car immediately began to go straight! The car literally changed direction by about 45 degrees! Other times, I have been in a car when it slid on ice. Suddenly the ice ends, and when the tires, which are going sideways, meet the pavement, there is always a jolt, because the tires are designed to go backwards or forwards, but not sideways. The great weight of the car, which the tires are carrying, causes a sudden impact which sometimes even results in the car rolling over, or a sharp impact before the car's sideways momentum stops and it begins to roll forward again.

That night there was no jolt, or impact at all as the car suddenly changed direction. What happened?

*He shall give His angels charge over thee, to keep thee in all thy ways. They shall hold you up in their hands.. (*Psalm 91:11–12)

With the cry of the name of Jesus, His Angel was sent, and gently redirected the car away from the ditch, to bring me home! Thank God there were no cars coming from the other direction, because I was in the other lane.

As the car resumed its straight path on the road, I slowed down and turned into the driveway. The tiredness I felt was quickly replaced by surprise and shock! I needed to get inside to kneel down and pray, because my heart was beating very fast from what had just happened. I parked the car, grabbed my things, and went towards the house. As I got out of the car, I heard within myself,

A thousand may fall at your side, and ten thousand at your right hand, but it shall not come near you . . .

I didn't understand why I was hearing this now. I went inside, threw down my things, grabbed the Bible, and knelt down to pray. The room was dark – the way I like it at night. As I began, I noticed car lights coming through the window. I looked out and noticed that in the same area where I had slid on the ice, there were two cars, which had slid off the road, and into the ditch! I looked again, and noticed that there were several other cars stopped, and they were getting out to help the drivers who had crashed. Knowing that someone was helping, I returned to my prayers. Shortly after this, I heard sirens, and emergency vehicles coming to help.

The Angel of God had come and delivered me from calamity. As I began to pray more, my heart returned to normal, and I thanked God for saving me, and for all that He had done in these special two days. Afterwards, I laid down and enjoyed a wonderful rest.

MIRACULOUS PRAYERS . . . IN ACTION!

Behold, I send an Angel before thee, to keep thee in the way, and to bring thee into the place which I have prepared. (Exodus 23:20)

This is a beautiful promise of God's protection. As the Israelites were preparing to enter the Promised Land, their Angel is given three responsibilities. –

1. to keep them safe on their journey

2. to prepare the final destination

3. to bring them to their destination

I know - whether I am driving at the hospital, Church, or just going about my personal matters – as God brings us to our daily destination He will also put someone there that needs help, and to hear about

God. This is our ministry. If we are in God's will, there will be someone that needs our help every day.

PRAY THIS MIRACULOUS PRAYER:

Lord Jesus! This is the day You have made – I will rejoice and be glad in it! Thank you for giving your angels special charge over me today, as I go out. Send someone to me, and I will help them in whatever way you so desire. I cover this day with the blood of the Lord Jesus Christ. Therefore, no evil will befall me all the days of my life. I will dwell in the secret place of the most High, as I both go out and come in .

In Jesus' name

The Spirit Himself Intercedes for Us

The Spirit helps us in our weakness. We do not know what we ought to pray for, but the Spirit Himself intercedes for us through wordless groans. (Romans 8:26 NIV)

There was a time I worked a lot with the owner of a bakery. I visited him 2 or 3 times a week. There was a lady working there who always greeted me when I came in, and was very kind. On a particular day, I noticed she looked sad, so I asked how she was feeling. She had been suffering with a severe cold for several weeks now, and was feeling very bad. I could see by her face that she was hurting and was very congested.

She let me pray for her. The presence of God was very strong as we prayed, and both of us felt it. The next day, I was at home, and was curious about her, so I called. She was very happy and shared some great news. After our prayer, she went home and looked in the mirror. There was something white in the back of her throat. Unable to reach it, she gargled with mouthwash. To her surprise, as she spit out the mouthwash, this white thing came out, which she described as a small ball of flesh! The moment she spit it out, her feelings changed completely- all the congestion left, and immediately she felt well again!

After this healing, several years went by. When I started to produce a DVD for my ministry, I thought of this unique healing. I got in touch, and she agreed to tell the story of how God had healed her through our prayer. When she stood in front of the camera, and began to describe what happened, tears filled her eyes.

The story was so touching, all of us began to cry. When I asked to pray for her, I had no idea how much she had suffered before this day. She kept the real story to herself, until it was time to record it on camera. Three years before our prayer, her throat and face became very swollen. After consulting doctors, she was advised that there was a serious thyroid problem, as well as a large lump which was extremely swollen.

The thyroid gland was removed, and she had radiation treatments to shrink the lump around her throat. After the radiation, she had to live isolated in her home for several months. A very expensive medicine was prescribed to treat her and hopefully, maintain her health. However, without insurance, the cost of the medication was too much for her. She decided to stop using the medication, and placed her faith in

God, believing Him to heal her.

Miraculously, God healed her. The functions of her body that were damaged by the radiation were healed, and worked perfectly, FOR SEVERAL YEARS. Unfortunately, in the month before we met in the bakery, the old symptoms had returned. Headaches, congestion, and swelling of her throat and face had come back with a vengeance. So, when I found her in the bakery she was really troubled.

Until she stood in front of the camera that day, I knew none of this sad story. In the bakery, my prayer was just a simple one, asking God to heal a woman suffering from a severe cold. We both found out that God knows all, and what is lacking in our prayers, He takes care of.

The Spirit helps us in our weakness. We do not know what we ought to pray for, but the Spirit Himself intercedes for us through wordless groans.

There is often much hidden beneath the surface! That is why it is important to know - we don't always know how we should pray! But the Spirit Himself is present to intercede and reach areas much deeper than we ourselves are aware of – Amen?!

When she told her full story, two years had passed, and her health remained perfect. We were all joyful to know the Spirit Himself had performed her final healing that day in the bakery!

MIRACULOUS PRAYERS . . . *IN ACTION!*

The Spirit helps us in our weakness. We do not know what we ought to pray for, but the Spirit Himself intercedes for us through wordless groans. And He who searches our hearts knows the mind of the Spirit, because the Spirit intercedes for God's people in accordance with the will of God. (Romans 8:26, 27 NIV)

Wow! Are you beginning to see the potential of the Spirit when we pray? What are the issues closest to your heart? The Spirit searches our hearts, and then intercedes for us according to the will of God.

Mark 5:33 describes a woman who had suffered terribly for twelve years -

She came and fell down before Him and told Him all the truth.

The moment she came to Jesus, she was healed and set free of all of her suffering.

PRAY THIS MIRACULOUS PRAYER:

Lord Jesus!

I open my heart to you this day. I lay everything before you. This moment, may the Power of the Holy Ghost touch me in my deepest places. I thank you that He ever lives to intercede for me. I am made whole!

In Jesus' Name.

You Have Turned My Mourning Into Dancing!

. . . thou has turned for me my mourning into dancing. . (Psalm 30:11)

God is God, because He is able to completely turn around desperate situations. I recently preached at a *Holy Ghost Night.* At the end of the service, He came and turned one woman's desperate situation completely around. The scripture came to pass as her mourning was turned into dancing!

The message was entitled, *A New Day,* coming from Genesis 1:2–5:

And the earth was without form, and void; darkness was upon the face of the deep. And the Spirit of God moved upon the face of the waters. And God said, Let there be light and there was light. And God saw the light, that it was good: and God divided the light from the darkness. And God called the light Day, and the darkness he called Night.

The message was that from the beginning of

time, the Holy Spirit has been the agent of change from darkness to light. At the beginning of the service, I asked the whole church to stand, and we all repeated this prayer:

Lord Jesus, today is a New Day – by the fire of the Holy Ghost, I drive out every power of darkness from my life!

Now that is an earth – shaking prayer! Excitement rose up immediately! The service was beautiful – about 3 ½ hours, with intense worship, many prayers, the message and the final invitation for personal prayer, to which all of the audience of almost 50 responded and came forward.

God visited the final prayers in a remarkable way. A woman came with such extreme leg pain that she was having trouble walking. She almost stayed home. At the end of the service, she came for prayer. Not knowing her, or anything at all about her, I asked what the request was. She simply said – *for a pain in my chest.* – for whatever reason, she did not say anything about her legs!

After praying, the Power of God caused her to fall to the ground. Some of the ladies kneeled down and continued praying for her. I felt a strange leading to take off her shoes! so I kneeled down, took them off, grabbed her two feet, and began praying for her. As I began to pray, I repeated, and shouted in a loud voice.

SURGING FIRE, SURGING FIRE, SURGING FIRE

71

THROUGHOUT YOUR BODY!

She began crying, and I saw her whole body begin to shake. Afterwards, she told me what had happened, and that after the prayer, she was completely healed! The following Sunday, she shared her testimony and performed a beautiful dance song to the Lord. The whole congregation was deeply moved to hear what God had done for her and see the beautiful presentation.

MIRACULOUS PRAYERS . . . *IN ACTION!*

Thou has turned for me my mourning into dancing (Psalm 30:11).

King David wrote this Psalm because when God turned things around, he was overjoyed! Let's look at two more:

Let Israel rejoice . . .. Let them praise His name in the dance. . (Psalm 149:2-3)

And David danced before the Lord with all his might. (2 Samuel 6:14)

David had reason to mourn. On a daily basis, there were attacks, deaths, pains and sicknesses, not to mention many wives, a large family, and the entire Kingdom of Israel to oversee. One can imagine his many burdens, which frequently caused him to mourn.

Yet he knew how to TURN IT ALL AROUND! I often see people who will stand completely still during worship, as if they are frozen. One thing I know – just like David, THAT IS NOT ME! I met this awesome God during worship, and that is one place I will always see my life turn around. Why not put on some nice worship music, and begin to sing and dance around a bit? See what God will do for you!

PRAY THIS MIRACULOUS PRAYER:

Lord Jesus! This body I occupy is the Temple of the Holy Ghost. Therefore, body, I command you, from the top of my head to the soles of my feet begin to rejoice in the Lord. As I begin to praise the Lord in the dance, may the Fire of the Holy Ghost set me free from deep within.

In Jesus' Name!

Let Everything That Has Breath Praise the Lord!

Let every thing that has breath praise the Lord. Praise the Lord. (Psalm 150:6)

Let everything that has breath praise the Lord! What a declaration! Have you ever noticed how birds start singing so loudly before daylight? And again, as the sun goes down, they intensify their song. They are fulfilling the mandate of God – to Praise Him!

We learn much observing how God operates through animals. A great lesson I learned recently was through a dog! I often consider the role of pets within the American family. Probably the most popular is the dog – *man's best friend.*

Recently my parents had to put their dog to sleep, because she was getting old, and having a lot of trouble walking. The final days were very hard for the whole family. It really saddened me to see them grieving the loss of a companion who had shared their lives for many years. I realized there were very strong ties between the dog and my parents, which left them feeling as if one of their own children had passed away.

I had been saying something jokingly for many years – Americans have two different types of children – the type with two feet, and the type with four! Pets often fill a void in the family. In times past, the family was closer, with many members living together. As it has broken down over time – often children and parents live apart. A void has appeared and is filled by - you guessed it – the dog!

A woman I have been mentoring for several years - Stacey, began to talk about one of her friends named Joanna. Stacey was telling her about the Love of God, and it was really touching her.

Finally, I got to meet her. They were very close friends, and coworkers. After speaking for a short while, I asked if I could pray for her. Joanna suffered with depression ever since her father died years ago. She really loved him, and still missed him, although he had been gone for many years. She had gotten married, but there was still a void in her heart, and as a result, it had grown into a depression which never seemed to leave her.

Before praying, the Lord told me that Stacey should stand behind Joanna because the Power of God was going to touch her. As we prayed, it happened just like that. For a time, she began gasping heavily, and crying. I realized that demons were leaving her.

Before we go any further, let me explain something concerning my ministry at this point.

Mark 1:25 – 27 reads as follows –

And Jesus rebuked him, saying, Hold thy peace, and come out of him.

And when the unclean spirit had torn him, and cried with a loud voice, he came out of him.

And they were all amazed, insomuch that they questioned among themselves, saying,

What thing is this? What new doctrine is this? for with authority commandeth He even the unclean spirits, and they do obey him.

When Jesus began his ministry, He started doing something that amazed those around him – casting out demons, and evil spirits. In this case, the spirit even cried out with a loud voice.

It was something new – *a new doctrine*, but we need to understand that it was a regular part of His ministry, and it is what distinguished Him. To many, it was new, amazing, and often beyond comprehension. Yet to others, it seemed absurd. Whatever we think about this, we need to realize that this was a part of the ministry of Jesus which is clearly recorded in the Bible. Even today, it is also a regular part of the ministry of true Ministers of Jesus Christ.

Luke 9:1 reads as follows:

Then he called his twelve disciples together, and

*gave them power and authority over all devils, and to
cure diseases*

You see, in Jesus' ministry, He trained and en-
abled his disciples to do all of the work that He did.
Casting out demons was a regular part of the disciples' ministry. As my ministry progressed, and God
sent a great man of God, Reverend Tony, into my life
as a mentor, this authority and power coming from
Jesus to his disciples was passed along to me through
the ministry of Reverend Tony. In years of training
with him, casting out demons has now become a regular part of my ministry.

So, to return to Joanna, I was very aware that demons were leaving her. Finally, a great calm came
over her after the demons had been driven out. It was
a very moving experience for all of us, and we really
felt the Presence of God.

For quite a while, Joanna composed herself, and
then told us she felt like a great weight had been
lifted. There was a joy she hadn't felt for many years!
It was beautiful, and one has to experience something
like this to understand how rich and holy the environment had become. None of us wanted to leave, and we
stayed around for quite a while, joking with each
other, laughing a lot, and greatly enjoying this special
moment.

Before we said goodbye, I made an appointment
to visit Joanna's house to pray with her whole family.

I advised Stacey to stay in touch with her to make sure that everything is ok, and that the devil does not try to come back and steal her blessing. Several days later, Stacey called to report that Joanna was very happy. God really touched her, but unusual things were happening in her house. The dog had begun to get very upset! *For the first time ever*, Joanna returned home, and found him running around, barking and very excited. In a rage, he tore the pillows to pieces and was even beginning to rip up the carpet!

When I heard this, I immediately remembered Mark 5:13

Forth with Jesus gave the demons leave, and the unclean spirits went out, and entered into the swine: and the herd ran violently down a steep place into the sea.

Intuitively, I knew the dog was sensing demons in the house! His behavior had suddenly become just like the scripture, when the swine *ran violently* into the sea. I was certain this is what was happening with him! I realized that animals often become violent in the presence of demons.

I was really looking forward to our meeting – though a bit uncertain about the dog – I did not want him to become violent around me! On the scheduled day, Joanna called to cancel. This further convinced me that the devil was really troubling this family.

Not long after, I visited Stacey at work, and discovered Joanna was there too. Her husband was waiting to take her home in ten minutes or so. I told Stacey I would like to pray with them before they left and went to wait in my car. To my surprise, I saw Joanna leave the building, get into the car and drive away with her husband. Stacey came and apologized to me, explaining that the dog was in the car, and after I arrived, he began getting upset, and barking. Not wanting to create a disturbance, they had left quickly.

It was clear to me now. The demon began to upset the dog the moment I arrived, causing them to leave in a hurry. I stayed calm and waited for the right moment to arrive – I knew this demon would meet his end soon enough. Perhaps a week later, the moment came! I arrived at the workplace and saw Eduardo standing beside his car. We had met on several occasions, so I went and talked with him. The dog, Coffee, was in the car. A bit uncertainly, I greeted the dog, knowing we would need to be friends! He was very friendly. I never touch dogs - but in this case, I made an exception and found a place behind his ears that he liked, and rubbed until I could see he was very happy!

Eduardo agreed for all of us to pray together. Several minutes later, Joanna came out, and we sat down to pray. Eduardo asked if he should bring Coffee. I said very affirmatively – YES! I didn't know what would happen, but I knew the dog needed to be present!

Eduardo sat next to Joanna, and I sat opposite the two of them. Joanna pulled Coffee onto her lap.

I began to pray, and almost immediately we felt the presence of God. I looked, and saw that Eduardo was holding her hand. I put my hand on top, praying more forcefully, and began rebuking demons. I had my eyes closed. I could feel Eduardo's hand underneath mine shaking. I continued to pray until I sensed a breakthrough, and calmness. Immediately after, I felt Coffee lay his head on top of my hand and rest it there! What a surprise when I opened my eyes and saw him resting his head on my hand – as if he was agreeing with our prayer.

I ended and could see that all of us had been touched by the presence of God! Eduardo described what had happened, because he was the only one with his eyes open. After the stillness came, Coffee turned his head, looking slowly all the way to one side, then all the way to the other. After looking both ways, he then laid down his head on top of our hands!

WOW!! What happened? Can you guess? Coffee had seen the demons being cast out and was looking to make sure they were all gone. Afterwards, feeling the Peace of God, he laid down his head to agree with us!

Let every thing that has breath praise the Lord. Praise the Lord!!

Go Home . . .
The Lord has had Compassion on Thee

He that had been possessed with the devil prayed that he might be with Him. Howbeit Jesus suffered him not, but saith unto him, Go home to thy friends, and tell them how great things the Lord hath done for thee, and hath had compassion on thee. (Mark 5:18, 19)

This is one of the most dramatic miracles in Jesus' ministry. In a great deliverance, a legion of demons are cast out of a man, he is restored to his right mind, and becomes a preacher of the Gospel! When Jesus is leaving, He instructs him,

Go home to thy friends and tell them how great things the Lord hath done for thee, and hath had compassion on thee. And he departed and began to publish in Decapolis how great things Jesus had done for him: and all men did marvel.

Because of Jesus' compassion, the man's life of torment is completely turned around! He began to go around the ten cities of Decapolis telling everyone of the great things Jesus did for him. This man was a terror to all, and only Jesus could end it and turn his life completely around.

He is described as follows:

Who had his dwelling among the tombs; and no man could bind him, no, not with chains: Because that he had been often bound with fetters and chains, and the chains had been plucked asunder by him, and the fetters broken in pieces: neither could any man tame him. And always, night and day, he was in the mountains, and in the tombs, crying, and cutting himself with stones. But when he saw Jesus afar off, he ran and worshipped him verses 3 – 6

What was his condition when Jesus found him?

• He was near death - living in the tombs, and suicidal – always cutting himself with stones.

• He had supernatural strength – as much as they tried to bind him with chains, he broke them and was untamable.

• Despite all the evil within him, he recognized Jesus, and even worshipped him.

One night I was in the hospital very late, on my way home. As I left, I heard the Holy Spirit telling me to go to the Emergency Department. (E.D.) Whenever He speaks like this, I go eagerly, knowing something great always will happen. On this night, I entered into the same environment as Jesus when He stepped out of the boat and met the man with a legion of demons.

The woman I was about to encounter this night

was very similar –

- she was near death, and suicidal.

- she had supernatural strength – the devil was present, and his evil power had taken control of her life.

- despite all the evil within her, she recognized, and had to submit to Jesus.

I entered the E.D, seeking the one I was sent to. As I got to room 12, I noticed a nurse sitting at the door, watching the patient. I looked inside and knew this was the one! There was trouble - she was lying across the bed in a peculiar position and the sheet had fallen off the lower part of her body. I asked if I could see her. It was ok with the nurse, but she doubted we would be able to talk because the patient was incoherent.

So she covered her up again, and I went in.

When I entered, this was my meditation:

Put on the Lord Jesus Christ (Romans 13:14)

This is a position of holiness, and also battle. Immediately, the God I know equips and prepares me to war and conquer the forces I sensed were troubling this woman. As I stepped in, there were strong smells of vomit, and she was wearing a hospital gown alone. Whatever clothing she was wearing had been removed.

Although the woman's face was attractive, now the demeanor was completely frantic. The medium length hair was completely disheveled. It seemed like all of the sterility of the E.D. was cancelled by the horrible odor of the vomit, which was coming out of this woman.

The moment I said I'm a chaplain, she came out of her stupor and became attentive. There were moments of clarity, but then she became very agitated. Restraints were on both her hands and ankles. Frantically, she tried to break loose, pointing to an imaginary shelf, saying she needed to get another beer. While thrashing around, the sheet kept falling off, exposing her again. Despite this behavior, she responded to my questions. When I insisted she lay back down on the bed, and remain covered, she obeyed.

In moments of clarity, she kept repeating . . .

I'm going to kill myself!

I'm going to kill myself!

She was very adamant about needing to end her life. She let me pray for her and remained calm. I grabbed one of her hands forcefully and commanded the murderous spirit to leave and stop tormenting her in Jesus' name. I prayed through the faithful scripture that has proven itself many times, and personalized it –

I shall not die, but live and declare the works of the Lord. (Psalm 118:17)

After the prayer, she was still incoherent, but

something had changed. She began repeating. .

I want to go back to the place in Westbury

This seemed to be some sort of rehabilitation program she was in before but fell back into alcohol abuse. I noticed she no longer talked about killing herself, or the imaginary beers, but was now eager to get help.

I was happy with the prayer, and how she responded. When I got home, the first thing I did was rinse out my nostrils. The offensive odor of vomit seemed to be like a presence which remained in my nostrils. I felt better after this. I prayed for quite a while. I had seen a lot – both good, and evil. After something like this, I needed to really seek the Lord, to clear my mind, and get peace. As I interceded for this woman, the Lord instructed me how to proceed:

Say to the prisoners, Go forth; to them that are in darkness, show yourselves. (Isaiah 49:9)

This spoke to me, and I formed a plan. I would help to get her out of the prison and darkness. I knew that God had already begun because of what was said about the place in Westbury. My goal was to see her through the hospital and placed in a good rehabilitation program.

DAY 2 TUESDAY

I discovered she had been admitted, but was heavily sedated, and sleeping. Again, the strong smell of alcohol and whatever else was in her system were present, showing me that there were a lot of poisons in her body. The different combination of odors was really offensive and made me more aware of the evils that needed to be driven out of her life.

I sat down beside the bed. Laying my hand on her head, I prayed quietly, but forcefully, until I felt a release from God, then left.

In the evening, I called to check, and they said she was still sleeping. Later, at home, I prayed again for her. God was really giving me a burden to continue praying for her, so He could bring a change.

DAY 3 WEDNESDAY

Today, she was finally awake. I had to introduce myself, because she didn't remember our first meeting. Her name was Linda. She started talking but was very uncertain about me. However, as I prayed, read Scriptures and sang, the Presence of God unfailingly began touching her.

When I returned later, she began to trust me and started opening up more. I explained that God had delivered me from drug problems, and completely changed my life around. As she began to understand this, hope came.

As a child, she suffered much sexual abuse. As an adult, these troubles led her into drugs, alcohol, prostitution, and working as a dancer in a night club. Despite this, she believed in Jesus, and desired to return to Him.

DAY 4 THURSDAY

Today, she was transferred to the psychiatric unit for detoxification. This was very hard, because the medication was making her drowsy and incoherent. Despite this, she shared with me her strong desire to go somewhere to receive help that would change her life. As we discussed the possibilities, I agreed to help her locate a Christian rehabilitation program.

Later, we met in the Quiet Room – a place used for visits with patients. We shut the door, and began to sing, and pray. I began to pray from Acts 1:8 -

You shall receive power after the Holy Ghost has come upon you.

As I began to pray, I expected the Holy Ghost to come in the same way as the first night when He visited me. The Power of the Holy Ghost indeed began to touch her, and she fell to the ground. I left her there for quite a while, and sat in a chair, singing, and allowing God to do His to work in her. She cried intensely while lying on the ground. Finally, she got up and sat in the chair.

Faithful is He that calls you, who also will do it (1 Thessalonians 5:24)

The God that visited me on a cold night almost 20 years ago had shown up again! Linda had been deeply touched, and for the first time, had a big smile on her face! We said goodnight, and I promised to return the next day.

DAY 5 FRIDAY

Today, I spoke with the social worker, and the rehabilitation center which we found, to begin the process of application. I also spoke briefly with her father. He was very happy and told me that this was an answer to their prayers.

DAY 12 FRIDAY

Today, Linda was finally released from the hospital and admitted to the rehab program. I am thankful to God. Once again, God has had compassion. I am happy to have seen His Power come and turn Linda's life around. Hallelujah!

MIRACULOUS PRAYERS . . . IN ACTION!

Go home to thy friends, and tell them how great things the Lord hath done for thee, and has had compassion on thee. (Mark 5:19)

Beloved, no matter how bad things are – God is always able to turn them around for the better. Why? His compassion!

Jesus cares about us–you see, the worse off we are, the more He intervenes and does great things! Consider this scripture: *The Spirit that dwells in us lusts to envy.* - (James 4:5)

This man had a VERY STRONG PERSONALITY. Given a chance, the strong lusts of the Holy Spirit will overpower the lusts of the devil. The result is that a person with a strong personality will do great things for God! . Consider the life of Saul – a man who hunted down early Christians and brought them to their deaths. He became a great evangelist named Paul, who planted Churches throughout Europe and Asia, and wrote two – thirds of the New Testament!

PRAY THIS MIRACULOUS PRAYER:

Lord Jesus!

Have compassion on me, and my loved ones. May your strong desire to change us overthrow all plans of the enemy. May your mighty Power deliver us from every bondage of evil today. Our lives shall become a testimony that You can turn around ANYTHING for your Glory.

In Jesus' Name

I Trust the Lord

He shall not be afraid of evil tidings: his heart is fixed, trusting in the Lord. His heart is established, he shall not be afraid, until he sees his desire upon his enemies. (Psalm 112:7,8)

A lady asked me to call her friend in the hospital who was 7 months pregnant. There was a blood vessel wrapped around her placenta, which was getting more dangerous as the delivery drew near. The doctors scheduled a Caesarean operation to deliver the baby safely and protect the mother from harm.

The mother was unhappy about this and asked me to agree with her in prayer for a normal, full-term delivery of the baby. We agreed, basing our faith on the following scripture:

Nothing shall cast their young, nor be barren, in thy land: the number of thy days I will fulfill. (Exodus 23:26)

After discussing this, I shared a story that came to mind. Many years ago, I had a pain which seemed to be sitting on my right kidney. Although it was not severe, it remained for a long time. Every time I sat down, there was an enlarged feeling within me that was uncomfortable. I chose to believe God would heal me, rather than seek medical help.

One night, I was in Church, and the Presence of God was very strong during the worship. The Pastor began to pray and asked everyone to hold hands. There was a man next to me who was BIG! He had huge hands like vice grips! When we began to pray, he became excited, and started jumping up and down, squeezing my hand. He squeezed so hard that I had to take it out quickly. When I shook my hand to relieve the pain, I remembered that one of my thumbs had been sprained. Earlier in the week, I had fallen and sprained it. I asked God to heal it, and then forgot, carrying on with the pain, but not concerned. As I shook off my hand, I remembered that the thumb was still hurting when I came into the service. But now, the pain was completely gone!

Shortly after this, the Power of God became so strong that I fell to the ground, and my whole body began shaking. Quite a while went by, and finally I came to myself. I dragged myself to the seat, feeling very intoxicated by the Presence of God. When I opened my eyes, I saw that many others were also on the floor, being touched by God.

The excitement in the Church was indescribable. I realized something else: for the first time in so long, the pain inside me was completely gone! I wanted to share this with the Church, so I wrote a note, and asked an usher to give it to the Pastor, who was still passionately praying.

The Pastor read the note, and announced to the Church, *"We are already receiving testimonies! Someone with a pain in their kidney has been healed!"*

Two days later, there was another service. A woman came up and began to speak – she was in Church when the Pastor read my note. That morning, she went to the hospital. The doctors had found a large stone in one of her kidneys a week before. When she entered the office prepared for surgery, the doctor made a request. He stated that he didn't usually do such things, but for some reason, he wanted to take another X-ray. He came out of the lab holding the two photos. Holding up the one from the previous week, he showed her the stone. He then showed her that day's x –ray, and where the stone was before - now there was none! He then declared

I don't know what happened – but the stone is gone! You can go home – we don't need to operate!

The woman declared –

I know what happened – God healed me!

The doctor, not believing in God, answered her –

Whatever! you can go home – we don't need to operate

The woman stood in front of the Church, holding up the two x – rays, as she told her story. The Church was absolutely crazy with excitement! As I shared this story with her, I could sense her excitement and increase of faith! We then began to pray, rebuking the devil that was putting her life at risk, and asked God to correct the blood vessel which was endangering her life.

During the prayer, I also boldy declared that the baby will be delivered full term, normal delivery within one week of the regular nine months required. A week after this prayer, I received a text message from the woman –

Good Morning Pastor, I am back in the hospital, the devil is a liar, please continue to pray for me. The Lord is able to deliver me

I responded,

OK, will call you a bit later

I was on my way to a Church Service, so I said a short prayer, and called her after the service. When she answered the phone, I knew she was excited! She began to tell me the good news: the previous night, she saw a bit of blood coming from inside, so she went to the hospital. As she arrived at the hospital, the blood had stopped; however, the doctors did a full examination and took an x – ray of the baby. To everyone's surprise, the blood vessel that had been dangerously wrapped around the placenta was completely gone! The doctor confirmed what our prayer had asked for – the caesarean operation was no longer necessary! The doctor cancelled it, and rescheduled a regular checkup, as the baby developed towards a normal delivery!

I am happy to say the miracle baby has arrived, and both mother and son are healthy, and happy that we all trusted the Lord. For the first time, I visited this mother, with her new baby, and family. What a joy it was to be together! It was as if we had all known each other for ever. For many hours we talked, laughed, sang and prayed together, as we celebrated the wonderful miraculous baby that God had given this family!

MIRACULOUS PRAYERS . . . IN ACTION!

He shall not be afraid of evil tidings: his heart is fixed, trusting in the Lord (Psalm 112:7)

What can we learn from this woman with such tremendous faith? Her trust was in THE LORD!

Is there something causing you concern? Continue to seek help, as she did from the doctors. Yet, her trust was not in them, nor in the uncertain solution that they presented to her. God always has a solution. In His word, a testimony such as the one which the woman connected to, or perhaps something He has done for us in the past. This is what we need to keep close to and believe wholeheartedly.

PRAY THIS MIRACULOUS PRAYER:

Lord Jesus:

I nail every evil report hanging over my life onto Your Cross. Therefore, it is taken away. Send your ministering spirits to change my situation into a glorious testimony.

In Jesus' Name!

Every Chain is Broken!

One day in the Rehab House a new resident was referred to me, whose name was Henry. As we started talking, he told me about his life – sexual abuse by stepmother and brother which resulted in HIV infection. Later he fell into crack addictions. He truly desired to serve the Lord but felt there were forces resisting him. He mentioned that God recently appeared to him in a vision, and said he had ONE MORE CHANCE, which is why he admitted himself.

Despite all his problems, most of his family were Christians, and they were all praying for him. Immediately it reminded me of Acts 12:5, and I resolved to read this story when our prayer time began.

Peter therefore was kept in prison: but prayer was made without ceasing of the church unto God for him.

I noticed he had *two* chain bracelets on his wrist. I asked him where he got them, and he said he pulled them out of the trash. I explained to him that they held evil spirits, and he should get rid of them. I read Acts 19:11, 12

And God wrought special miracles by the hands of Paul: so that from his body were brought unto the sick handkerchiefs or aprons, and the diseases departed from them, and the evil spirits went out of them.

I explained the scripture in the following way: because the devil was originally in Heaven praising God, he knows all about Him, and how He works. The devil is a great imitator of God, only uses it for evil.

You see, in this scripture handkerchiefs or pieces of Paul's clothing contained a special power transmitted by him which were used to heal the sick and cast out evil spirits. The devil, as an imitator, uses certain items like clothing, jewelry or charms to transmit evil spirits and harm people. This was how I perceived that the two bracelets that he was wearing were cursed.

Immediately, he told me he wanted to be obedient and would get rid of them. To my surprise, he grabbed them, and with one hard pull, broke them both off, and gave them to me to dispose of! After a few minutes, we ended our conversation, and began to pray, because I was already feeling the anointing very strongly.

I began by reading from Acts 12. As I read the whole chapter, I knew that this was going to be a tremendous deliverance! I got to verse 6 and 7 which read as follows,

. . .the same night Peter was sleeping between two

*soldiers, **bound with two chains:** and the keepers before the door kept the prison.*

And, behold, the angel of the Lord came upon him, and a light shined in the prison: and he smote Peter on the side, and raised him up, saying, Arise up quickly. **And his chains fell off from his hands.**

When I got this far, I had to stop! We both looked at each other in amazement as the Presence of God began to touch us. I did not remember this part about

Bound with two chains, . . . and his chains fell off from his hands!

It was a beautiful confirmation that God would set him free this day! We began to pray. After a few minutes, I told Henry to stand up, close his eyes, lean his head back and breathe deeply, focusing on Jesus. I told him not to speak, that the conversation was no longer with him.

I began his deliverance, and, under inspiration of the Holy Ghost, prayed as follows -

You demon, I command you to speak and come out of this body in Jesus' name!

I began rebuking the demons. After a while, all of his upper body began to convulse, and make unusual movements. I knew they were beginning to leave. A voice spoke and said two times,

I will not leave! I will not leave!

I got more violent in my prayer, and after a few minutes the demon said,

I am gone! I am gone!

Immediately, Henry's body stopped the convulsions, and I sensed the Peace of God coming into him. I shouted, *you are free!* After that, I blew a blast of breath on his face, and the Power of God knocked him down. I held his hands, and guided him into the chair, where he fell, with his neck leaning back on top of the chair. He was immobile for a few minutes. After he came to himself, he smiled, and we both praised God together and sang a song!

We both knelt down together, and I asked him to thank God for what was done. He prayed passionately for about 5 minutes, and then we both sat down. He was a completely changed person – free, happy, and wonderfully at peace!

MIRACULOUS PRAYERS . . . *IN ACTION!*

The Spirit of the Lord God is upon me; because the Lord has anointed me to preach . . . the opening of prison to them that are bound. (Isaiah 61:1)

You see, in this example, the dear brother was imprisoned by the devil: drug addiction, childhood abuse, and many other things. One of the most important things to know is that Jesus came with a very clear mission:

For this purpose the Son of God was manifested, that He might destroy the works of the devil. (1 John 3:8)

99

Where have you been bound? in sickness, addiction, sin, relationship problems, or anything else? I pray today the Lord would set you free in the exalted name of Jesus!

PRAY THIS MIRACULOUS PRAYER:

Lord Jesus! Today, I acknowledge that I am bound by (name your situation) Forgive me of my sins. I renounce any covenants I have entered into with the devil, whether willingly, or unwillingly. I recommit my life to you Lord Jesus; I am yours forever. I break this bondage off of my life. I invoke the Power of the Blood of Jesus Christ to come and set me free this day. Today, I am free to serve God totally.

In Jesus' name

Doctor Jesus

I will not bring on you any of the diseases I brought on the Egyptians, for I am the Lord that healeth thee. (Exodus 15:26)

Another man at the Rehab Center was suffering a lot of pain in his shoulder. More than 10 years ago, Christopher had an accident at work; doctors had done surgery, but it never fully recovered. It seemed like the pain was getting worse. He was having trouble sleeping and could not lay on the shoulder. Every time he rolled over, it hurt him. When I asked him how high he could lift his arm, he showed me – the highest he could go was exactly perpendicular, 90 degrees out from his shoulder. Because of the pain, he could not lift it any higher. Unfortunately, because he didn't have insurance, he could not have the x-ray that he so much needed to get further treatment.

Christopher is a man of great faith, who has a loving, and intimate relationship with God. The relationship has deepened considerably since he came to the house. However, his knowledge of the Bible is very little. I asked him if he knew any scriptures about God's ability to heal. His answer was no.

We then looked at the following scriptures:

I will put none of these diseases upon thee, which I have brought upon the Egyptians: for I am the Lord that healeth thee. (Exodus 15:26)

I then began to explain this to him. You see the word *that healeth thee* comes from the Hebrew, *rafa* – meaning physician, or healer. This is the same word in the Hebrew language for doctor. So, what this is saying is, I am the Lord, your doctor. To understand this better, let's look at another scripture –

Jesus said unto them, Verily, verily, I say unto you, Before Abraham was, I am. (John 8:58)

What Jesus is saying here is that He has been before Abraham – He is the I am. So, when we put these two together, we can understand Exodus 15:26 in a different light –

I am Doctor Jesus!

We then looked at Acts 10:38:

How God anointed Jesus of Nazareth with the Holy Ghost and with power: who went about . . . healing all that were oppressed of the devil

We need to understand something clearly –

sickness is an oppression of the devil!

It is certainly NOT God's will for His people to be sick! Hebrews 13:8 declares –

Jesus Christ the same yesterday, and to day, and for ever

According to this, everything that is written about

Jesus in the Bible is STILL IN EFFECT, and will be forever!

As we spoke, I summarized for Christopher –

·God spoke to Moses a promise which we fully understand now – I am Doctor Jesus

·When Jesus came, He had Power and the Holy Ghost to heal all sickness, which comes from the devil

·Jesus is the same today – He is our Eternal Doctor who is always able to destroy every sickness of the devil and bring healing.

Afterwards we prayed. I asked him to lift his arm now. Immediately, he lifted, and it went all the way above his head, and moved freely in all directions! In addition, all the pain was gone!

HE WAS TOTALLY HEALED! we went around the whole campus, showing everyone how he was before, and after God healed him. What a day of celebration! Glory to God!

MIRACULOUS PRAYERS . . . IN ACTION!

*I am the Lord that healeth thee. (*Exodus 15:26)

Thank God for doctors, and medicine! Through them our quality of life has improved tremendously, as well as our life expectancy. However, it is God Almighty who gives the knowledge and resources to make it possible for them. Modern medicine was unavailable to this man. There were no doctors available. So, it was simple for his faith to receive healing from Jesus. Why was he healed?

·because of His deep love of God.

·because his faith was the only alternative to pain.

Once he heard the Word of God, his faith IMMEDI-ATELY received the healing. We need to develop passionate faith in Jesus as our Doctor, who has come to destroy every sickness of the devil in our lives. Doctors often play an important part in our healing, but we need to know that they are secondary to Jesus. From the days of Moses, God's infinite Power has been available to heal His people. Will you receive it by faith today?

PRAY THIS MIRACULOUS PRAYER:

Doctor Jesus!

I come to you today needing healing. Sickness comes from the devil. I set myself TOTALLY to resist it! I reject it altogether, and command it to leave this body NOW. This is the temple of the Holy Ghost. May your Power fill me today and heal me.

In Jesus' name

Love Never Fails

Love never fails (1 Corinthians 13:8 NIV)

One night, I went to visit a man that was sick. We did not know each other. When I said I am a Pastor, his whole demeanor changed. He began to sweat and appeared very uneasy. Despite his feelings, he very much wanted to talk. Often, the Presence of God immediately touches others, and the most important things come to light. His reactions proved this. The Holy Spirit within me brought conviction to him, and the sin in his life was exposed without words – the result was evident in his uneasiness.

And when He comes, He will convict and convince the world and bring demonstration to it about sin . . . because they do not believe in Me . . . But when He, the Spirit of Truth . . . comes, He will guide you into all the Truth (John 16:8, 13 AMP)

My first question was - how have you been feeling lately? His response hit me like a bomb! He said lately he had been very tormented – trouble sleeping, scared about his whole situation, the sickness, and felt like he might be near the end of his life.

His biggest regret was never having given his parents grandchildren to enjoy, because most of his life he had been a homosexual. That was when the bomb dropped! I had been around a few homosexuals before, and I always felt very uncomfortable. However, this was before I became an ambassador for Jesus Christ.

Several thoughts went through my mind before responding. The first was my initial memory of previous encounters, and I remembered the scripture that was spoken to the men of Israel, which is very clear about this lifestyle –

You shall not lie with a male as one lies with a female; it is an abomination. (Leviticus 18:22)

Yet, as I thought a bit more, the Holy Spirit reminded me of another verse – *Love never fails (1 Corinthians 13:8 NIV.)* I quickly realized that it was not for me to judge this man, but rather to present the Love of God as a solution to his torment.

I realized that as he considered the end of his life, the reality of Heaven and hell were drawing near. The Holy Spirit was really guiding me along now, so I asked if I could read something from the Bible. He agreed, and I read the following –

And one of the malefactors which were hanged railed on him, saying, If thou be Christ, save thyself and us. But the other answering rebuked him, saying, Dost not thou fear God, seeing thou art in the same condemnation? And we indeed justly; for we receive the due reward of our deeds: but this man hath done nothing amiss. And he said unto Jesus, Lord, remember me when thou comest into thy kingdom. And Jesus said unto him, Verily I say unto thee, Today shalt thou be with me in paradise. (Luke 23:39–43)

After this, I said a few things –

Listen, no one knows when we are going to die – tomorrow, 10, 20, or 70 years from now.

Let me explain something, I am very confident that I am going to live a long, healthy and prosperous life because the Bible promises, *With long life will I satisfy him, and shew him my salvation.* (Psalm 91:16)

Yet, I didn't want to say to him that he might die tomorrow, so I stated it in a less threatening way that I thought he would receive well. *"Listen, no one knows when we are going to die – tomorrow, 10, 20, or 70 years from now. However, when that day comes – wouldn't it be nice to know that you will be in this Paradise that Jesus spoke about?*

The man very eagerly shook his head, and said, *"yes – I would really like to be there!"*

So I told him it would be very easy, and asked if he was willing to say a few prayers together he would be assured of an eternal home in Heaven – or Paradise, as described in this scripture. He very enthusiastically agreed, and we began to repeat a prayer which was something like this –

Lord Jesus, thank you for your Love towards me. I

come to you today as a sinner. I renounce all of my sins. I reject every covenant I have made with the devil – whether knowingly, or unknowingly. I ask you for for-giveness today from all of my sins. Today I make a new covenant with you through the blood of the Lord Jesus Christ. May your Love come from Heaven today, and heal me of all my pain, sorrow, hurt and sicknesses. Help me to live a holy life before you from this day for-ward. I ask you to give me your Holy Spirit. Today, I confess and believe that I am born again. Today, I ac-cept you as my Lord and Saviour. Today, Heaven is my eternal Home. In Jesus' Name.

As we finished the prayer, many tears were com-ing down, and he had a big smile on his face. The transformation was tremendous, and we both were very happy as we spoke a few minutes more. He gave me a big hug and I left, promising to see him a few days later.

The next time I visited him, he was very happy, relaxed, and excited to see me. He thanked me repeat-edly for the visit, and prayer. He also said that he had been sleeping peacefully for the first time in many years. Finally, he was feeling very good about his life. One might say this man was born as a homosexual. Well, we found the answer to his birth problem – get born again! The prayer we said together could be called a "born again" prayer. His physical and emo-tional torment was ended on the day that he was spiritually reborn.

I am sure the angels in Heaven were celebrating that day because hell had been robbed of a prisoner, and Heaven had received another eternal saint!

MIRACULOUS PRAYERS . . . *IN ACTION!*

Love the sinner, hate the sin is a common phrase. When I met Jesus, it was the Love of God working through His people that brought me to Him. My grandmother never said anything about my sinful drug habit. The friend who brought me to Bible study, and Church, though he must have smelled the marijuana on my breath, never said a thing, and neither did the pastors and elders of the Church when I began coming. Consider this scripture –

Ye are the temple of God . . . the Spirit of God dwelleth in you. If any man defile the temple of God, him shall God destroy; for the temple of God is holy, which temple ye are. (1 Corinthians 3:16)

If we defile our bodies with drugs, or homosexuality, do you think one sin is worse than the other? I don't think so. As I reflect on this man's salvation, and my salvation, there are a few things in common.

· Our sin was known to the person who presented the Gospel.

·There was no judgment, condemnation, or even mention of our sin.

·The Love of God was demonstrated in both word

and action.

·The Gospel message and salvation from the Lord Jesus Christ was accepted and brought a tremendous transformation to our lives.

You do well when you complete the Royal Rule of the Scriptures: Love others as you love yourself . . . Talk and act like a person expecting to be judged by the Rule that sets us free. For if you refuse to act kindly, you can hardly expect to be treated kindly. Kind mercy wins over harsh judgment every time. (James 2:8,12&13 MSG)

PRAY THIS MIRACULOUS PRAYER:

Lord Jesus –

Today, I recognize you as the King of kings, and Lord of lords. I accept my job as your Royal Ambassador with all of my heart. I will reflect your Love in thought, word and action. I reject every evil accusation and lie of the devil which would cause me to condemn anyone. Today, may I be merciful, and know that You will always help me to win others to your Eternal Kingdom. Anoint my heart, mind and tongue with Grace abundant. Thank you for the Power of your Love which never fails.

In Jesus' name

SPIT - HEALING MINISTRY! !

*He spit, and touched his tongue (*Mark 7:33)

I first heard the term, spit – healing ministry from a famous preacher. He spoke one night about a crusade he led in Korea. During the crusade, they brought a woman that was deaf and dumb for prayer. As the woman stood before him, the Lord spoke to him in an unusual way.

Spit into her mouth, and I will heal her!

I can imagine some of your reactions right now! I was shocked too, but we should understand this command from the Lord is not so unusual if we know the Gospels! Jesus used his spit to heal many! For example, in Mark 7, Jesus spits on his finger, and touches the tongue of a man that is both deaf and dumb. Immediately, his tongue is loosed, and he speaks.

However, with several thousand people in the audience, can you imagine the things going on in the preacher's mind when the Lord instructed him to do this? Lord, was that really you speaking? Imagine the Lord doesn't heal her. Violent massacre of famous evangelist!

Not wanting to disobey the Lord, he told the entire audience, the Lord said He will heal her if I spit into her mouth! The woman stood before him, and opened her mouth wide, inviting him to spit into it! He made a loud noise, clearing his throat, and spit forcefully into her mouth. Immediately, she was healed and began screaming in a loud voice! The whole stadium went crazy praising the Lord!

I always remembered this testimony when I read Mark 7. However, for many years, it remained just a memory.

My entrance into the spit healing ministry happened quite suddenly and unexpectedly late one night. I went to meet a woman who asked me to visit and pray for her. I had never met her before and decided to go and meet her. I arrived at about 7:15 and left just before midnight. During my final prayer with the woman, we discussed the scripture –

Upon Mount Zion, shall be deliverance, and there shall be holiness, and the house of Jacob shall possess their possessions. (Obadiah 17)

We prayed for quite a while, sitting at the kitchen table. Towards the end, I grabbed her hand and began to pray for her deliverance. Immediately, she began coughing, and holding her throat, as if there were something hindering her breathing. I could tell those evil spirits were beginning to manifest in her chest and throat by how she was reacting. I began to pray through the scripture –

He has swallowed down riches, and he shall vomit them up again: God shall cast them out of his belly. (Job 20:15)

She started choking and looked at me. I looked around, and saw no water or glasses, but here on the table was the bottle of water I had been drinking. Although it is not my custom to share my water with others, I remembered the scripture –

He spit, and touched his tongue (Mark 7:33)

In a split second, I recalled this scripture, and the preacher's testimony. My Faith gave me the OK, and I gave her my water to drink, believing that my own saliva would do the same as in the case of Jesus and the preacher.

She drank it down quickly, and to my surprise, immediately ran to the bathroom, shut the door, and began to vomit for 4 or 5 minutes! As she vomited, I heard loud screams, as demons were leaving her! Several days later, to my fascination, this woman explained something to me. Before our meeting, she had eaten a good dinner. Interestingly, she told me, what she vomited was some strange substances, and NONE OF THE DINNER SHE HAD EATEN! Now, it has been many years since this deliverance, and she has become a great friend of mine, and a faithful member of our ministry. This event marked the beginning of a major turnaround in her life.

Perhaps 1 ½ years later, I was in a Prayer Service on a Saturday morning. There were about 6 of us, each taking our turns for prayer. I listened while everyone prayed, and the Holy Spirit really brought to my attention one woman's prayer, who had asked the Lord to set her free from her smoking habit.

After everyone was done, I started to pray, and began to pray through a message from Haggai 2:6,7

For thus saith the Lord of hosts; Yet once, it is a little while, and I will shake the heavens, and the earth, and the sea, and the dry land; And I will shake all nations, and the desire of all nations shall come: and I will fill this house with glory, saith the Lord of hosts.

My interpretation of this scripture is that when the Glory of God comes down, every evil power - whether in the heavens, earth or under the earth - are all shaken, and driven out of the believer's life. The Glory of God fills us and brings healing and deliverance!

While I was praying through this topic, the Lord told me that I should call the woman forward who had asked to be set free from her smoking habit. I had a small bottle of water that I had begun to drink from. He said when I gave her my water to drink, she would be set free. I remembered instantly my previous experience, and did not hesitate.

The woman came forward, and after I explained

what the Lord had told me to do, without question, she took the water and began to drink. It happened so quickly! Thank God someone came to stand behind her. The woman leaned her head back, and the water went down her throat instantly. Before she even finished, the Power of God touched her, and she fell to the ground. It was quite a sight to see; the woman falling backward, with the bottle still in her mouth ! I quickly grabbed the bottle, as the other woman held her, and laid her down to the ground. I instructed the Church to begin praying for her. We prayed violently for her, rebuking the demons of death, addiction and smoking. Immediately, her stomach and legs began moving in a very unusual way, as the demons began to manifest within her. Her head went back, her mouth opened wide, and all of us watched in amazement, as she exhaled heavily several times. The evil spirits left, and then she remained absolutely still, as her deliverance was complete. By the time she was ready to get up, she was feeling very intoxicated in the Spirit. To this day, as far as I know, she has never gone back to smoking again!

MIRACULOUS PRAYERS . . . IN ACTION!

Are you struggling with addiction of any kind? Alcohol, smoking, drugs (legal or illegal)? What about food? Addicted to sweets? caffeine? Salty food? Junk food? Gluttony? Is there sickness in your body?

PRAY THIS MIRACULOUS PRAYER:

Lord Jesus!

(Pray like this:)
As I hold up this water to Heaven, may your Healing Power enter into it right now.

As I begin to drink this water, may everything planted by the enemy be consumed by fire. I command the evil spirits causing (name your affliction) to leave my body now in the name of Jesus. Let every unhealthy desire be taken away from me now forever. By the Power of the Holy Spirit, may I be completely healed today. I praise your Holy Name.

In Jesus' name
Drink the water now!

A New Thing

In November of 2018, the Man of God, Reverend Tony returned to New York for a visit. As always, I was excited to see him, looking forward to my time with him, and serving as his Personal Assistant.

One of the things I enjoy most about being with him is travelling to different Churches and hearing his preaching. I know that for every trip to NY, both he and many of his Church leaders in Nigeria Fast and Pray extensively. As a part of this consecration, the Lord always gives him a special message, which he usually preaches several different times while I am with him. On this visit, the message that the Lord gave him was,

Behold, I will do a new thing; now it shall spring forth; shall ye not know it? I will even make a way in the wilderness, and rivers in the desert. (Isaiah 43 :19)

When I heard this message, I spoke to the Lord, and said AMEN ! Something deep inside of me was touched. Remember the verse says, now it shall spring forth. It was springing forth from inside of me, without a doubt, and I was ready for that new thing, even if I didn't know what it was!

Although my life in NY was good, and I had a lot of great things happening in the Ministry, for me it was a hard place to live, and in addition, the cold winters were more and more troubling as each year went by. I was ready for a new thing, even if I didn't know what it was!

One of the things that needed help was our local Church. For several years, both Reverend Tony and I had started a fellowship in Mount Kisco, but for one reason or another, it wasn't growing at all. While he was there, someone introduced me to a nearby Pastor, who had a large Spanish speaking Church. He agreed to speak with both Reverend Tony and I about the possibility of helping us to start a Spanish – speaking branch of our Church in Mount Kisco.

When we went to meet the Pastor, one of the first things that he did was to invite me to a three-day conference in Puerto Rico the following January. The seminar was entitled Church Planting and Leadership. Honestly, what excited me the most was this: PUERTO RICO! ! ! Yes, I needed to learn a lot about Church planting and leadership, but what excited me was . . . PUERTO RICO! ! !

Trying to maintain a professional appearance with both Reverend Tony and the Pastor, I contained my excitement. He assured me that he would find someone for me to stay with in Puerto Rico, because I knew absolutely no one.

In the car ride home, I asked Reverend Tony what he thought about the trip, and he said, yes it sounded like a good idea.

Meanwhile inside I was shouting, PUERTO RICO! ! ! By Faith, I decided that I had to go. Even if I didn't have the money for the flight . . . by Faith; remember the message I had been hearing? I WILL DO A NEW THING! Eventually, the money came to buy the ticket, and I decided, no way am I going to Puerto Rico and returning back to NY in the cold month of January after only 3 days! I bought a ticket for two weeks, although I didn't know anyone, what I would do, or even where I would stay after the Conference was over. That New Thing was springing forth like never before!

The conference was great, and I learned a lot. But what was greater was the people! I began to fall in love with Puerto Rico, because of the people! As a foreigner, I was treated with more respect than I ever had received in NY. The friendships and kindness I experienced in those two weeks created in me a strong desire to return to Puerto Rico. I left knowing that God had started a new thing and Puerto Rico was the place that He would do it.

Let me explain something about Reverend Tony. His Senior Pastor is known as the Prophet. All of the Grace, Giftings and Blessings that Reverend Tony has, the Prophet has in even greater abundance. I have met the Prophet, and he has ministered to me several times over the years. An encounter with him is always Miraculous. Reverend Tony always comes to NY under the delegated authority of the Prophet.

On my last night in Puerto Rico, I had a dream. In the dream, I was in my room in NY. The Prophet came into the room, and wanted to sit down on the couch, but he couldn't because it was cluttered with too many things. So, he prepared to leave, and told me, put your house in order . . .

I puzzled over the dream, because I am always a neat person, and the couch is never cluttered with things. What I perceived he was telling me was - close out your affairs in NY, it's time to move to Puerto Rico.

I returned to NY and began to Pray. I prayed, and I fasted until God answered. How God answered was he showed me some of the drug addicts I had seen in Puerto Rico, so desperate for help. When I prayed, I began to hear the words . . . A New Life. I began to see the beautiful Mountains of Puerto Rico, and a vision to open a Ministry of Rehabilitation for Men in the Mountains of Puerto Rico began.

A few months later, I returned to Puerto Rico, A HAPPY MAN! This time I was going to stay for six weeks. The vision God gave me was slowly coming together. I began to form a Non – Profit Ministry, named A New Life Men's Center, and not sure where to begin, but with a lot of Faith, I began sharing the Vision and speaking to many of my new friends. A friend from my first trip allowed me to stay in his house for two weeks, until he left for a vacation in NY. He took me to his Church one Sunday, and the Pastor allowed me to speak briefly about my vision of A New Life Men's Center. Later, back at my friend's house, he became a bit concerned because I hadn't yet found a place to stay when he left for NY. He called one of his Church members who lived nearby and had a large house with a complete apartment downstairs that was empty. When he asked the man if I could stay with them, unfortunately, he said no, because they didn't know me well, and weren't comfortable having me in the house. My friend became a little discouraged and went into the other room to watch TV. Several minutes later, I heard his phone ring, and he began talking to someone, but I didn't hear him very well. Soon I heard a loud shout from my friend, Hallelujah, thank you, Lord, I love you! You answered my Prayer! He came into my room very excited and told me what happened. After speaking to my friend, the man told his wife about the request. The wife surprised all of us! When she heard me speaking in the Church that morning, she told her husband, the Lord said to her, that is a Man of God, and he will stay in your house! Hallelujah! After hearing this, the husband called my friend again, and said, it would be fine if I stayed with them!

This couple have become great friends, and a tremendous blessing to my life. When I moved to Puerto Rico permanently in October of 2019, they allowed me to stay in their house for over a year.

Now, as I sit down to finish this chapter, I have lived in Puerto Rico for over four years. I really thank God for the new thing He has done for me and A New Life Men's Center, as well as all the new things He has yet to do. We have purchased a beautiful property in the Mountains of Puerto Rico. Our first buildings, a Sanctuary, and Bathroom are almost finished, and soon we will be having special Inauguration Services to dedicate the Sanctuary to the Lord and recognize the many who have enthusiastically helped us with this project. Plans are being made for the construction of future buildings necessary to open the Rehabilitation Program.

MIRACULOUS PRAYERS . . . IN ACTION!

Remember ye not the former things, neither consider the things of old Behold, I will do a new thing; now it shall spring forth; shall ye not know it? I will even make a way in the wilderness, and rivers in the desert. (Isaiah 43:18 & 19)

Today, perhaps you want something more out of your life. Maybe you don't know exactly what you want, just something more, and something better.

PRAY THIS MIRACULOUS PRAYER!

Lord Jesus!

I come to you today. It is time for something new in my life. You know the desires of my heart, and what is best for me. I demolish everything from my past that has held me down. They are gone and forgotten. Precious Holy Spirit, begin now to release that new thing into my life in a mighty way. Send new people and resources to me that will make it happen. It is done. Hallelujah! I now move in Faith to work with God and see that New Thing come into my life In Jesus' Name

Doing Good and Healing the Oppressions of the Devil, from Near and Far

I went out one morning to look for a piece of property in the mountains of Puerto Rico. The land was not far away from where I lived, but I didn't know the area at all. A friend recommended a surveyor who would help me to survey the land, if I decided to buy it. The property belonged to a family, but all of them were either dead, or lived far away. The executor of the property was a nun who lived on the other side of the island and wasn't able to tell me much about the location of the property, since she had moved away from it many years ago.

Anyway, the Surveyor and I set out to look for the property and arrived at the approximate location in about 15 minutes. After about half an hour of enquiring with various residents of the neighborhood, we finally found a dirt road going into a jungle at the end of the housing development. Fortunately, we found an elderly man living near this dirt road. He confirmed that the land was indeed further up the trail, but he didn't know exactly where it was. He advised us not to go and search, because no one had been up there for many years, and the road was hopelessly over-grown. If we were genuinely interested in finding the land, he recommended that we speak with a man named Freddie, who lived near to the entrance of the road we had come in on. Freddie had worked on the property many years ago, when it was an active farm. He was now a mechanic, so it would be easy to find him – the yard with all the cars near the entrance from the main road. If we could talk with him, he would surely show us where the property was.

We found Freddie's house, with all the cars, but he was not there. The surveyor spoke to his wife, Cristiana, who was very sad. I listened to the conver-sation but remained silent. She told us that her hus-band had been gone for about one month. He had taken their daughter Janine to a Treatment Center in San Juan and was staying with her and taking care of her there. Janine was in her early twenties, but she had a rare form of cancer, which required a special-ized treatment, offered by this Center in San Juan, supposedly the best in all of Puerto Rico. The mother was very upset, because after about a month, the treatment was still continuing, and the doctors were not offering much hope for Janine. In addition, she had been left with the two younger children to take care of. She did not work, and was very sad, because their only source of income had stopped, while her husband was away, unable to do his normal mechanical work. Cristiana was not sure when her husband would be back but ensured us that we could check back at any time.

We left Cristiana, not feeling very hopeful about the property for sale, or for her family, and their daughter Janine. Immediately, in the car ride home, the Holy Spirit began giving me that burden that I know so well.

I got home in the evening and finished up my work for the day. As soon as I began to pray, I knew that I had to go back and talk to Cristiana VERY SOON.

The next morning, I woke up and prayed my usual Prayers. He told me today was the day to go visit Cristiana, and I should bring her a gift. So, I went to the ATM and took out some money to give her. By God's perfect timing, a dear friend of my Ministry had recently given me some money, with instructions to help someone in need here in Puerto Rico. When I put the two monies together, I was happy to be able to have a generous gift to help Cristiana and her family.

I stood outside her house and called her. Within a few minutes, she came outside, and we stood talking by the side of the road. It made me feel sad to see her, and I understood the feeling of Jesus when he saw the sisters of his friend Lazarus who died.

Jesus wept. (John 11:35)

I asked her about Janine and her husband, and she told me that she was doing ok, but the doctors had not said if she would be able to come home soon. Again, she mentioned how things were so hard without anyone working in the family. I told her that I wanted to pray for Janine, but before, I have a gift to help her family. When I handed her the envelope, she started crying for a while, and then did something so beautiful! Standing alone by the side of the street with her, she gave herself the biggest hug and looked at me with great appreciation! I almost cried myself, it was a very special moment. I knew what the Apostle Paul meant when he wrote,

It is more blessed to give than to receive. (Acts 20:35)

I was really blessed that moment, but little did I know of the many more blessings on the way! We prayed together, for Janine's healing and for all of the family. Cristiana was deeply touched by the prayer. Again, she gave herself a big hug, and said many thanks, and I left to go home.

About a week and a half later, I went back to see Cristiana. To my surprise, her husband was home working again, and Janine was home again too! Hallelujah! The doctors had sent her home because the cancer had gone into complete remission! We talked for a few minutes, and Janine came out of the house, very nicely dressed, and was briefly introduced to me, and left quickly on her way to work. What an exciting day for me to see such a beautiful, healthy young lady, completely restored, and strong to work.

Several months went by, and I became busy with other activities. I decided that the property we looked at was probably not such a good idea, because of the remote location, and the amount of work that would be necessary to make it suitable. One day, I went to the local supermarket to buy a few things. I stood on the checkout line behind a man with a grocery cart that was full to the top with various food and house-hold items. The woman beside him spoke to him, and left him, apparently looking for something else. The man turned briefly to look at me, and I remembered him immediately. I asked him, aren't you the me-chanic named Freddie? He said yes, and we shook hands. His wife came back, greeted me and this time, gave me a big hug. They informed me that yes Janine, and all of the family were healthy and doing very well. We spoke for a while, both checked out, and said goodbye. I went into my car and began to say PRAISE THE LORD ! ! ! What a joyful moment! I had met this family several months ago, in a real crisis. A daughter in her early twenties, struggling with cancer. The fa-ther was unable to work, because he needed to care for her, and struggling to keep the family fed because of this situation. Now to see that God had healed her, she was living the life that He designed for her, and today, they are returning home with a car full of food and supplies for the family. I have to say that God is Great, indeed!

MIRACULOUS PRAYERS . . . IN ACTION!

How God anointed Jesus of Nazareth with the Holy Ghost and with power: who went about doing good, and healing all that were oppressed of the devil; for God was with him. (Acts 10:38)

The centurion answered and said, Lord, I am not worthy that thou shouldest come under my roof: but speak the word only, and my servant shall be healed.

And Jesus said unto the centurion, Go thy way; and as thou hast believed, so be it done unto thee. And his servant was healed in the selfsame hour. (Matthew 8:8 &13)

We can learn a few things from the above scriptures about Jesus' Healing Ministry:

1. An important part of Jesus' Ministry was DOING GOOD. He loves to help those who are in desperate situations

2. Jesus is able to end the oppression of the devil and bring Healing

3. He is able to Heal someone that is a great distance away, and to do it immediately.

When we learn to do good things for someone, and pray for them also, God can do great things. In the case of the Centurion, and his sick servant, he had the Faith that Jesus's Word was enough to heal the servant who was far from them. As Jesus spoke to him, the servant was healed!

PRAY THIS MIRACULOUS PRAYER:

Father in Heaven: Empower me to continue the mighty Healing Ministry of Jesus Christ. I bind up the devil and destroy all of his forces of oppression. Holy Spirit, lead me to those ones who need your goodness, healing and deliverance. Help me to generously bless those that around me who have great needs. Use me to do great Miracles

In Jesus' Name

Divine Liver Surgery

Several years ago, I received an email from a woman in Australia. She was concerned about severe pain in her liver and had gone to the doctor for an ultrasound. She had heard me preaching and saying prayers on a radio show and wanted my help. As I read her email, I knew that I could help her. We arranged a phone call. When I spoke with her, I began to ask her a few questions. I found out several things: she had been sexually abused as a child, and after that had several relationships outside of marriage. She also had been having dreams for many years in which she was attacked by either a red bear or a big black snake. We discussed several other things, however, from the moment I read the email, a scripture had come to mind. After talking with her, we looked at the scripture, and I explained a few things. Let's look at the scripture first:

And behold, there met him a woman with the attire of an harlot, and subtil of heart. . . Till a dart strike through his liver; as a bird hasteth to the snare, and knoweth not that it is for his life. (Proverbs 7:10–23)

What happened in this Scripture? It describes a

young man who is enticed by an immoral woman, and eventually becomes fatally hooked, and on the way to death. How this related to the woman from Australia was simple. There was sexual immorality in her past, and as a result of that, demons of sickness had lodged themselves in her liver, like the darts spoken of in the Scripture. We went through a series of Prayers, and the Presence of God touched her immediately. The pain left instantly. When she went back to the doctor, they performed another test, and the tests confirmed what we knew already: The liver was perfectly healthy, and God had healed her.

The Bible talks about something called Gifts of Healing

For to one is given by the Spirit . . .the gifts of healing. (1 Corinthians 12:8-9)

After understanding the revelation of this Scripture, and hearing the woman's testimony, I added this gift to my toolbox, ready to take it out as soon as someone else came along with a similar problem, and see God heal them as well.

Sure enough, in Puerto Rico, I began working with a dear friend who was suffering discomfort in her liver area for many months. She had gone to the doctor recently, and the diagnosis had really scared her. Tests revealed that her liver had begun to fail and was at Stage One. She was terrified because the doctors told her that if this continued, Stage Four would be fatal. I shared the testimony of the woman from Australia with her. We then prayed a series of Prayers. I put my hand on her liver and prayed towards the end. Afterwards, she was surprised to tell me that for several hours afterwards, there was consistent pressure, and constant heat on her liver, like someone was pressing against it. The Bible tells us,

And now, Lord, behold their threatenings . . .by stretching forth thine hand to heal; and that signs and wonders may be done by the name of thy holy child Jesus. (Acts 4:29-30)

Again, the Lord had done it for this beloved friend. The hand of the Lord had literally touched her for several hours, performing her divine liver surgery, and removing every threat and evil arrow of sickness. She was very confident, and several weeks later, I went with her to a follow up visit with the liver specialist. Again, the doctors confirmed that her liver was perfectly healthy, and the failure had completely stopped! Praise the Lord!

MIRACULOUS PRAYERS . . . *IN ACTION!*

And now, Lord, behold their threatenings . . .by stretching forth thine hand to heal; and that signs and wonders may be done by the name of thy holy child Jesus. (Acts 4:29-30)

Now, I want to speak to anyone with a past, and anyone with some type of sickness in your body. When I say, someone with a past, it should be clear, many of us have had former relationships outside of marriage. What we should realize from these two cases is that when this happens, something is literally deposited into our bodies, that can result in later sickness. If that person is you, It would be good to say these Prayers. Depending on the seriousness of the sickness, it might even be necessary to Fast and Pray. But please know that God is able to heal you.

The above Scripture describes threats of the enemy. We must know that often sickness comes and threatens our lives, our thoughts and emotions, and if not dealt with, can even kill us. But as we have seen in these two cases, God is able to stretch His Hand of Power and perform the Miracle of Healing.

PRAY THIS MIRACULOUS PRAYER:

Father, in the Name of Jesus Christ, I come to you in Faith for my Deliverance and Healing. Today I confess all my sins, and repent of any sexual immorality in generations past, and in my own life. (place your hand on the area of sickness) Today I rebuke every unclean spirit causing this infirmity, and command them to come out right now. Every evil covenant of my life is now broken. I come to you now Jesus and ask you to cleanse and heal me. I renew my Covenant with you through your precious Blood. May the Power of the Holy Spirit run through my body right now, from head to toe, and heal me and set me free.

Conclusion

By now, we understand the Power our prayers contain, and how instrumental they are towards getting miracles from God. After looking at many different testimonies and Bible promises, we are on our way to praying in a way that shakes the kingdom of darkness and moves the miraculous hand of God to action.

In closing, let's look at two more scriptures which will help us to receive many more unique and spectacular miracles than we ever believed possible.

Very truly I tell you, whoever believes in me will do the works I have been doing, and they will do even <u>*greater*</u> *<u>things</u> than these, because I am going to the Father.* (John 14:12 NIV)

In this verse, Jesus is telling his disciples they will do even *greater things* than Him – *things more extraordinary and more wonderful!* That is a tall order. It is a charge for us to *expect spectacular miracles.*

When Jesus went to the Father in Heaven, He sent the Holy Spirit to come live inside us. The person of Jesus Christ, in the form of the powerful Holy Spirit, lives inside of each of us. This is what makes these *greater things* possible! Because He lives inside of us, let's go forward expecting *spectacular miracles*! Now to the final scripture –

This is the disciple which testifieth of these things . .

And there are also many other things which Jesus did, the which, if they should be written everyone, I suppose that even the world itself could not contain the books that should be written. Amen. (John 21:24, 25)

What is the Apostle John talking about here? Jesus did so many wonderful things that the world cannot contain all the books that would testify of them. As we go about doing *greater things* than Jesus, we should also expect to *fill the world with more miracles than can be counted!*

To close, let's pray this final *Miraculous Prayer* –

Lord Jesus –

As I go forward, by the fullness of the Holy Spirit, may spectacular miracles increase in my life. May they not only be astonishing to all, but so many, that they cannot be counted. I believe it, so be it done for your everlasting Glory.

In Jesus' name

Endorsements

That which was from the beginning, which we have heard, which we have seen with our eyes, which we have looked upon, and our hands have handled, of the Word of life (1 John 1:1)

This beautiful book is a clear declaration of what the great Servant of God, Michael Blacker, has seen, and his hands have handled. It is not a story or hearsay. It is a first hand account of the manifestation of God's Grace and Glory. Well crafted, designed and written for the purpose that you and I may know that indeed God is still in the business of healing, deliverance and break-through. It is my prayer that as you read this book, you will be able to access the divine truths that are so clearly stated in this book, and your life will not remain the same— in the might name of Jesus.

Michael Blacker is a man I know very well—a great servant of God who has the zeal and great desire for the Power and the move of the Spirit in this end time. He is a prayer machine—he loves praying and staying in the Presence of God through regular fasting. The many nuggets available in this book are the more than 15 years of his WORK with God. As you read I be-

lieve you will begin to experience the fullness of God's Glory in Jesus' name. Indeed— you shall not die, but live and declare the works of the Lord. I highly recommend this book

God bless you!

Reverend Anthony Oghre

Secretary to the Ministers' Council World Evangelism Bible Church Worldwide

Coordinator World Evangelism Bible Church USA & Canada

District Pastor Surulere District, Lagos, Nigeria

Michael Blacker has a sincere love for God that is evident in his ministry and writings. In this book he shares with you his heart for God and his unshakeable faith that has seen God really answer prayer. May his experiences of miracles and healings encourage you, deepen your faith and give you hope that God is with you for truly nothing is impossible with God!

Lori Torrano

Hospital Chaplain

As we draw closer to the last days before Messiah's return, the Kingdom of G-d must arise from within us to demonstrate its power to a lost and dying world. Not only is Yeshua's Power evident in Michael Blacker's life, but you will be encouraged to learn how to apply it to your own walk through some of his incredible experiences and powerful prayers. He has moved out in faith, believing the word of G-d and applying it wherever he goes. This is truly Prayer in action! A real faith builder!

Reverend Grant Berry

Senior Minister and Messianic Author

Messiah's House and Reconnecting Ministries

In seven years with our ministry, Pastor Michael has helped many treat the roots of their problems, receive freedom and return to their families usefully whole. I am excited about Miraculous Prayers. His ministry of healing has been a blessing to all of us at Pivot. In times that darkness seems to cover the earth, this book is a powerful tool which will bring God's healing to people of many nations.

Reverend Richard T Williams, Director

Pivot Ministries, Inc.

Men's Drug and Alcohol Rehabilitation Ministry

A NEW LIFE MEN'S CENTER

Puerto Rico today has great need of a strong and well-structured Drug and Alcohol Rehabilitation Program which will help solve the chronic problem of addiction among the many men of the Island, and produce future generations of productive, sober men and families. A New Life Men's Center is a program currently under construction on a beautiful farm in the Mountains of Puerto Rico. Very soon we will be opening our program to serve the men of Puerto Rico, their families, and eventually those of many other nations.

To help build our program or for further information contact us at: anewlifemenscenter@yahoo.com

 @Pastor Michael Blacker

www.ingramcontent.com/pod-product-compliance
Lightning Source LLC
Chambersburg PA
CBHW070750120626
46557CB00002B/537